How To Be A Goal-Getter

How To
Be A Goal-Getter

A Biblical Perspective on Achieving Your Goals

Melissa M Simon

Copyright © 2019 Melissa M Simon.
All rights reserved. This book or any portion thereof may not be reproduced or used in any manner whatsoever without the express written permission of the publisher, except for the use of brief quotations in a book review.

Scripture taken from the Holy Bible, NEW INTERNATIONAL VERSION®, NIV® Copyright © 1973, 1978, 1984, 2011 by Biblica, Inc.® Used by permission. All rights reserved worldwide.

Scripture quotations marked (NLT) are taken from the Holy Bible, New Living Translation, copyright ©1996, 2004, 2015 by Tyndale House Foundation. Used by permission of Tyndale House Publishers, a Division of Tyndale House Ministries, Carol Stream, Illinois 60188. All rights reserved.

Scripture taken from the New King James Version. Copyright © 1982 by Thomas Nelson, Inc. Used by permission. All rights reserved.

Printed in the United States of America

First Printing, 2019

ISBN 978-0-578-61003-0

Published By:
Simon House Publishing, LLC
Georgetown, KY 40324
www.SimonHousePublishing.com

Book Cover Design & Assistance:
Simon House Publishing, LLC and Claudia Wilburn

Dedication

MY DEAR HUSBAND, I dedicate this book to you and Milania. I love you so much. I am beyond blessed that God brought us together and have kept us growing stronger & closer than ever before. I thank you so much for your love, support, and your confidence in my vision. I truly am blessed to have such a God-fearing and praying husband. I love you beyond words.

MY DAUGHTER, MILANIA, My sweet baby girl. I dedicate this book to you and your father as you both have served such an amazing purpose in my life. I am blessed to have you and I am praying that we will raise you well to serve the Kingdom of God. You bring so much joy to our lives. Your desire to sing praise songs and worship at such as young age amazes us. We know that God will use you in a mighty way and we believe in all that you will do.

MY EDITOR(S) AND FRIEND(S), JACKIE COLE AND VANNAH BRAMMELL, I could not have completed this book without you. I thank you so much for your time, commitment, and energy while editing and revising my book. You have challenged and encouraged me to complete this God-driven goal of mine. I am forever grateful. I am blessed beyond measure to have dear friends and most importantly, sisters in Christ, for life.

Contents

Intro: Pursuit of Purpose .... Page 7

Chapter 1: God-Driven or Selfish Ambition? .... Page 12

Chapter 2: Called to Bear Fruit .... Page 37

Chapter 3: Determine Your Goal:
Commitment, Consistency, and Christ .... Page 53

Chapter 4: Be A Good Steward of Your Goal .... Page 73

Chapter 5: Pursuit of Achieving Your Goals:
Submit, Rely, and Obey .... Page 96

Chapter 6: Goal Building Blocks .... Page 116

Chapter 7: Watch God Work .... Page 127

Chapter 8: What if goals *don't* get achieved?
(Like you expected) .... Page 136

Outro: Summary and Encouragement .... Page 149

Intro:

THE PURSUIT OF PURPOSE

"I press on toward the goal to win the prize for which God has called me heavenward in Christ Jesus."

Philippians 3:14
NIV

INTRO: THE PURSUIT OF PURPOSE

Millennials are a generation seeking to make an impact, hustling like no other, and driven by their pursuit of purpose. Whether or not you fall into this generation, you can learn a thing or two from this ambitious crowd. *Now, I may or may not be a bit bias since I'm at the prime age of thirty and pretty much land in the middle of this demographic *queue hair flip*.* However, regardless of Millennials' tenacious drive, *I won't cut my generation any slack.*

I have come to realize that a huge driving force behind their ambition is heavily fueled by social validation and popularity. The desire to achieving goals appears to be for the purpose of *"one-upping"* each other. It almost feels like people are rushing to post their accomplishments just to receive praise and recognition that is greater than their fellow peers. It's unfortunate there is such a self-centered approach, even despite majority of Millennials classifying themselves as followers of Jesus Christ.

Fifty-six percent of Millennials consider themselves Christians yet an astounding fifty-three percent of them say they almost never or seldom read scripture[1]. *Hold up now. Say What?* The fuel to our faith comes entirely from God's word! *"So then faith comes by hearing, and hearing by the Word of God"* (Romans 10:17 NKJV). Now this isn't necessarily referencing *literal* hearing such as simply listening to The Word being preached but more of the exposure of God's Word whether through listening, reading, and/or studying. How can we be sure we are in alignment with God's will if we don't know what His Word says?

In this book, I want to target the concern of how this driving force of society, *or better yet, let's rephrase it as 'the world's"* pursuit of purpose, is impacting today's believers. How can we as believers be sure that we are not pursuing goals fueled by social validation and selfish ambition? How can we be sure the goals we wish to achieve are truly in alignment with God's will? Is there a way to harmoniously balance ambition and submission?

How to be a Goal-Getter: A Biblical Perspective on Achieving Your Goals will help you align your goals with God's will for your life. Throughout this book Biblical stories will be discussed, scripture will be referenced, and practical tools and wisdom will be provided to help you become a Goal-Getter, God's way.

The foundational scripture of this book is Philippians 3:12-14.

> *"Not that I have already obtained all this,*
> *or have already arrived at my goal,*
> *but I press on to take hold of that*
> *for which Christ Jesus took hold of me.*
> *Brothers and sisters, I do not consider myself*
> *yet to have taken hold of it.*
> *But one thing I do: Forgetting what is behind*
> *and straining toward what is ahead,*
> *I press on toward the goal to win the prize*
> *for which God has called me heavenward in Christ Jesus."*

Philippians 3:12-14 NIV

I want to explain this scripture a little more. *Watch out now, Meli is gonna school you on some theology. So get ready.* The apostle Paul wrote the book of Philippians approximately sixty-one years after the death of Jesus Christ. Paul wrote a letter to the church of Philippi, fueling their faith during heavily oppressed times.

He encouraged them to respond with joy while sharing his own struggles and hardships. *Let me add,* Paul was writing this letter from a Roman *JAIL*. And if you've read majority of the New Testament,

Paul wrote *a ton* of his letters from jail. *I mean, he was in jail like "fifty-leven-million" times! Okay, not that much* but he was in jail like *'all da time.'* But this was only because he was preaching the Good News of Jesus Christ when it was still forbidden in many areas.

Now specifically in this set of scripture, Paul was encouraging this group of people to not lose hope. To not give up. To continue to *'press on.'* To what though? To pursue Christ and to continue knowing Him on deeper levels.

Paul's sincere outpour is for us to *know* Christ, to *be like* Christ, and to *have the mind of* Christ no matter what. Essentially that is what our primary goal will be through our journey: to know Jesus Christ and to be one with Him. Much like an athlete in training, we must utilize discipline and self-control to break free from anything that would distract us from being an effective Christian. Through our specific journey of determining and pursuing our goals, we will set out to grow in our faith, align our desires and goals with His will, and walk in obedience to His commands. I want to provide some literal comparisons from the above referenced scripture on our pursuit of becoming a Goal-Getter:

Verse 12: **"Not that I have already obtained all this, or have already arrived at my goal, but I press on to take hold of that for which Christ Jesus took hold of me."**

As you go through the process of determining and achieving your goals, do not look at your goals solely as destinations or "stopping points." Instead, allow those goals to become building blocks to even larger goals. Because of that, we *must* continue to press on. Desire to grasp the goals God intends you to pursue, much like Christ desires to grasp all of our hearts for a daily pursuit of Him.

Verse 13: **"Brothers and sisters, I do not consider myself yet to have taken hold of it. But one thing I do: Forgetting what is behind and straining toward what is ahead..."**

Regardless if you have obtained an intended goal, keep moving forward and do not become stagnant. Don't let the past hold you back from moving forward, whether you are celebrating an old victory or paralyzed by past mistakes or negative mindsets. God desires to shape our character to become more and more like His Son, Jesus, throughout our journey.

Verse 14: **"*I press on toward the goal to win the prize for which God has called me heavenward in Christ Jesus."***

We are encouraged once again to '*press on.*' Our prize is not simply to achieve goals to receive praise, recognition, or bragging rights. The pursuit of goals that are in alignment with God's Will will serve a greater purpose for the full Glory and Honor of Him. We can rest assured that as we strive to be a Goal-Getter, based on Biblical principles, our faith will be strengthened, and we will truly feel fulfilled by serving the Kingdom of God.

Say it again. *Goal-Getter.* Now doesn't that sound fancy? Like you deserve a badge with that title or something? Well since I do think it deserves *something,* on page 166 there is a certificate intended to be copied and kept as a reminder of your commitment to be a Goal-Getter. Be prepared to work hard and reflect as you read through and utilize the chapters in this book.

We won't always be following trends or gain popularity from the world. We won't always be following trends or gain popularity from the world. But rest assured that none of your work will be in vain. When your intention is to be in the Will of God, He will surely be well pleased, and we can expect the bearing of good fruit as a result.

Chapter 1:

GOD-DRIVEN OR SELFISH AMBITION?

"For wherever there is jealousy and selfish ambition, there you will find disorder and evil of every kind."

James 3:16
NLT

GOD-DRIVEN OR SELFISH AMBITION?

When it comes to balancing ambition and submission, I find myself still having to check my heart and my motives. Just like the comedian-gone-potential-rapper, Jon Christ along with DJ Mykael V and Nobigdyl say in their song "Check Your Heart," *"You should check your heart with a stethoscope, lookin' up to God, He my antidote."* Now, if you've never heard that song before, reading those lyrics typed out probably sounded *super corny* but the song is actually catchy and *might I add* clean enough to blast around the youth at church camp.

But in all seriousness, you always have to check your motives. Are your goals God-driven or are they motivated by selfish ambition? Back in the day, if you had told me to evaluate my motives and ask why I was so goal-oriented, I wouldn't have thought anything was wrong with my ambition. My answer most likely would have been, "I just want to be successful." But if you kept prying and asking me, "But, why?" You better believe I'd give the same answer over and over just with some extra 'tude attached to it. *I mean, who really enjoys repeating themselves, anyway?*

Before I surrendered my life to Christ, I always described myself as: *Ambitious, Determined,* and even a *Workaholic*. I loved climbing the corporate ladder and I found the most value in life by holding a prestigious title. Anytime an interviewer asked what my top priority in life was, my answer was always "My Career." *Wow, talk about trying to get interview brownie points, huh?* Well, honestly, that's really what I valued the most.

I reflect back and can remember a stage in life where I was so proud of my success and achievements. I remember explaining to someone: "*I* worked hard for this! No one gave it to me. Everything *I* have was because *I* worked hard and it wasn't handed to me!"

Whoa now. I don't how I didn't realize there were some deep-rooted issues hidden between those passionate, yet aggressive statements. But if we aren't intentional about self-evaluation then we may not realize we have an issue with our ambition.

Now, there's nothing wrong with working with excellence and desiring to succeed in areas of life because that truly does bring glory to God. But we need to evaluate the driving force behind that motivation and realize there could be a deeper 'root issue' of your ambition that might not be in alignment with God's Will.

THE ROOT ISSUE

"But if you are bitterly jealous and there is selfish ambition in your heart, don't cover up the truth with boasting and lying."

James 3: 14 NLT

As an adult, I realized the root issue of my goal-driven tendency was based on issues from my childhood. I grew up emotionally distant from my parents, which developed into my adulthood as distrust for people.

In my adolescence, I desired to do well in school so that my mom would be proud of me. I strived for accomplishments because I felt I had to do well to earn her love. That was when I received the most praise and felt the most love from her. My parents divorced when I was six, and at the time my dad was serving in the Army. He was stationed in several places, so he was not physically in my life until my teenage years. I formed an opinion about my dad based on my mother's projected emotions and I never truly *felt* like I had a dad since he was absent from my life.

It was when I was a teenager that I decided to move with my dad since my mom and I had issues getting along. My dad was remarried by then and unfortunately, I didn't get along well with my step-mom either. They eventually had a son and I felt left out and neglected.

I moved back with mom after a few more years since I still couldn't seem to get along well with my dad and step-mom. I lived with my mom for a short period of time, graduating high school, and moving back with my dad since I decided to go to college in that state.

Then at the age of nineteen, I moved out on my own. I was working two jobs while going to school full-time. My mom was gracious enough to buy furniture I needed, while my dad supplied me with a cell phone and a car financed in his name. My daily expenses such as food, gas, utilities and rent were all taken care of by me.

I was working hard and providing well for myself until a year after I was on my own. My dad and step-mom had to file bankruptcy. They decided not to keep the car that I was driving and even decided to remove me from their cell phone plan to save money. Since I wasn't very emotionally connected with my parents, the way I felt loved was being provided for. When I felt they weren't concerned about my wellbeing, I became extremely hurt and more issues of distrust grew deeper into my heart.

After getting the car and cell phone taken away, I knew that I had to figure out a solution. I immediately got preapproved for a car, financed a brand new 2013 Chevy Malibu, and got my own cell phone plan. The world might praise someone who achieved so much for themselves at the young adult age of twenty-three but that very same boastful perspective caused me to put more hope into myself rather than God.

The lack of trust from my parents, caused me to guard my heart. Combine my distrust and my self-sufficiency and what do you get? A young lady who viewed hustle and ambition to the be the true solution to lack of provision in life. Again, the thought that I was the sole provider in my life, not God, grew even deeper. My boyfriend at the time loved my ambition (*and might I add, he is now my beloved husband. Awww. Cute, huh?*) He knew I was a hard-working woman and admired that about my character.

Unfortunately, my deep-rooted mindset to supply for myself caused tension once we got married. It was hard for me to allow my husband to supply things for me. I was trying to live adjoined with my spouse yet as R&B Artist Ne-Yo describes it as *"Miss Independent."*

As great as hard-work, effort, and ambition might sound, because I was not reliant on God and merely put trust in myself, I always felt a heavy burden on my shoulders. I felt like no one could help me and that I had to do everything on my own. I had a great deal of pressure to perform well professionally but also to take control of every single area of my life outside of my career. Yet essentially, reflecting back on those moments, I set that up for myself. I wore the badge of honor of independence, self-sufficiency, and the lack of trust for people for many years. I was using my accomplishments and selfish ambition to fulfill security in my life. But that was something only God could truly provide.

I always had an acknowledgement of God and was told Jesus Christ died on the cross for my sins. But I didn't truly understand what Jesus death on the cross actually meant. And I never knew that we could have a personal relationship with Him. I grew up going to church on Sundays and didn't think there was anything in our daily lives that needed to be done. The only time I thought about prayer, was to pray when something *really bad* happens and hope for a good outcome. But other than that, I felt no true dependency upon God or felt confident that He would hear or listen to my prayers.

The only way I broke past this self-ambitious cycle was hitting roadblocks in my career. I kept climbing the corporate ladder that eventually would come to a halt. The block in my career caused me to be frustrated and restless. No matter how hard I hustled or strived, certain doors just wouldn't open regardless of what I did.

I wish I could say I easily learned that God had full control and was the ultimate provider in my life, but because I was stubborn and had developed really deep-rooted issues of distrust and self-sufficiency, I experienced two or three more career plateaus in what I like to think was an effort for Him to capture my *entire* heart and to receive my *full* surrender.

Each roadblock seemed to soften my heart. It was in the broken moments that I sought God, repented of my behavior, and eventually came to realization that He was my ultimate provider in life, not me.

John Piper describes the process of God's miracle work of softening hearts as this, "God causes it [the miracle of unhardening], and I act the miracle of unhardening. God is the decisive cause, but my acting is a real, essential part of the miracle taking place."[1]

Another thought comes to mind, the scripture Ezekiel 11:19-20 NLT, *"And I will give them singleness of heart and put a new spirit within them. I will take away their stony, stubborn heart and give them a tender, responsive heart, so they will obey my decrees and regulations. Then they will truly be my people, and I will be their God."*

God ultimately is the one who changes and transforms our hearts, but it is through our action of repentance and surrender that the work can actually take place.

"Or do you despise the riches of His goodness, forbearance, and longsuffering, not knowing that the goodness of God leads you to repentance?" (Romans 2:4 NKJV). God blessed me with many career opportunities and He was the one who truly provided the provision.

He desired for me to acknowledge Him through those blessings, yet I put my hope and faith in myself instead.

I couldn't view my relationship with my parents and assume my relationship with God would be the same. My heart was damaged, bitter, and hurt from my experiences in childhood, but it was the transformative power of Jesus Christ who softened my heart. I began to realize that my parents never intended to cause the effect that took place in my childhood. They were simply making decisions they felt were best at that time.

I realized how short I come up in life trying do all things by my own efforts. The beautiful thing is, God never intended for me to do so. He never intended for me to bear the burden of life on my own shoulders. That's exactly why God sent his Son Jesus Christ to die on the cross. He became the ultimate sacrifice through His perfection and His holiness. Because Jesus died for me (*and for all*), He bore sin, shame, and guilt, to declare victory through His blood covenant. I don't have to look to myself for security and provision, instead I can find confidence knowing that it is all provided from Him.

Earning prestigious titles or obtaining positions of power to provide security and comfort in our lives will always cause us to strive selfishly. The only way to feel true and real security in life is found in our identity in Christ and who He is within us.

REFLECTION

- What is the motivating factor to the goals you have set?

- How does your relationship with your parents impact your view of God?

- Do you have an *"inner root"* issue that you may need to take before the Lord and ask for forgiveness of? God is faithful to forgive and He will restore and heal you in response to your repentance.

- Evaluate where you are in your life:

  - Where do you want to be and how does it align with knowing Christ more?

  - Where in your life have you hit a plateau? Think through how you got there and what your next step should be in light of God's desire for you to know Him better.

  - Have you sought God in your decision making and plans?

KNOW YOUR IDENTITY

"So you have not received a spirit that makes you fearful slaves. Instead, you received God's Spirit when he adopted you as his own children. Now we call him, 'Abba Father.'"

Romans 8:15 NLT

I *know*, you may want to rush and begin determining and pursuing your goals. *Trust me.* When I want something, I usually want it, like, *'yestaday.'* But it is vital to understand *who you are* as a Child of God and to know your identity in Christ before we are able to determine if our goals are truly God-driven and in alignment with His will.

We can easily lose a grip on our identity because the world has made us believe we identify through things such as our career, economic status, race, ethnic culture, sexual preference, gender, or even political party. Yet as believers we should first and foremost identify as a Child of God over anything else.

When we receive Jesus as our Lord and Savior we are immediately saved (see Romans 10:9). And in that exact moment, we receive the Holy Spirit (see Ephesians 1:14). Salvation is not earned, you simply just need faith to believe in Jesus Christ. In this, you receive the free gift of salvation from God and now have direct access to God the Father through His Son (see Ephesians 2:18, John 14:6, Hebrews 10:20, 1 John 5:20).

Because we have God's Spirit, *The Holy Spirit*, we have the ability to have a deeper and more intimate relationship with our Creator. We shouldn't just view Him as a far away eternal being. He should be viewed as your Father, *Abba Father.*

When you truly view and acknowledge yourself as *God's child*, your confidence in your walk with Christ comes from God's power alone. My daughter, for instance, knows that I am her parent. When my husband and I go to pick her up at daycare, she recognizes who we are and runs up to us. She is secure in knowing that she belongs to us. Because she feels this security in being our child, if we were to go to an unfamiliar place, she would seek comfort and protection from us and trust that we would provide that for her.

I wish I could add to this list that she would obey, *but y'all*. She's two and a half… and if you have children of your own, you know that obedience is not quite their top priority at that age just yet. *Pray for us!*

As mentioned before, I couldn't view the relationship with my parents the same way that I viewed my relationship with God. God is perfect. He is love. He is filled with grace and mercy. And although, over time, we will be shaped and sanctified to be more and more like Christ, we unfortunately will *never* be perfect.

Whether our parents were amazing God-fearing people who provided a great example of God's love for us or whether they didn't know God and caused a lot of hurt and pain growing up; we have to seek an individual relationship with Him and not bring any bias into our view of who our Heavenly Father is.

I often think of the scripture in Matthew 7: 9-11 NLT:

"You parents- if your children ask for a loaf of bread,
do you give them a stone instead? Or if they ask for a fish,
do you give them a snake? Of course not! So if you sinful people
know how to give good gifts to your children, how much more will
your heavenly Father give good gifts to those who ask him."

This scripture truly shows the heart of God, our Father. He is not selfish, not begrudging or stingy, and we don't have to beg or grovel when we come to Him with our requests. He is a loving Father who understands, cares, and comforts. If humans can be kind, just imagine how God, Our Father, who *created* kindness can be?

Before I developed a relationship with Christ, I always felt something was missing. I thought that it was the next accomplishment or the next promotion, but once I received those 'things,' I still didn't feel fulfilled. It was because the security I placed my hope in, was not just in myself, but the world too. I would have always been on a journey of 'bigger and better' and never truly finding it if I didn't realize having a personal relationship with Jesus Christ was my missing 'thing.'

I sought a relationship with Christ by finding a good church that preached inspiration from the Bible and helped me understand about God's grace and love. I grew more inspired to seek eternal things rather than temporal things like professional advances. It took time for me to develop a daily habit of prayer and reading the Word, but each time I committed to doing those things, it deepened my relationship with Him and helped me grow more secure in my identity.

As my faith grew, the desire to follow God's commands grew more, too. It wasn't just about following His rules but it was more about pleasing Him and knowing it was in reverence to who He is. As your relationship with Christ grows, you will develop a deeper desire to be where God wants you to be in life. Through that growth you will also grow in your submission to Him as well.

If we are going to be Goal-Getters, through Biblical principles, we have to know our identity in Jesus and be willing to submit to His path and His plans. We will evaluate this a little deeper in the later chapters. But now, we need to make sure we know and believe we are a Child of God above anything else.

REFLECTION

- What do you currently identify yourself as?

- After providing insight about identifying as a Child of God, how does that impact your view on your identity in Christ? What does it personally mean to you?

- Did the information in this chapter challenge your view on how you identify yourself? Why or why not?

- What ways are you seeking to develop or continue deepening your relationship with Jesus?

DON'T WASTE EFFORT BUILDING YOUR OWN KINGDOM

> *"For his Spirit joins with our spirit to affirm that we are God's children. And since we are his children, we are his heirs. In fact, together with Christ we are heirs of God's glory. But if we are to share in his glory, we must also share in his suffering."*
>
> **Romans 8:16-17 NLT**

Another way to be sure we removed all selfish motives is to identify *who* we are building for. When I discussed this topic of the world's view to pursue its own interests rather than God's, to Jackie Cole, a dear sister in Christ, she phrased it perfectly, *"Selfish ambition is like building your own kingdom rather than God's."* Wow. I never thought of it like that.

We can waste so much energy and time trying to lay down bricks to build our **own** kingdom when all we need to do is come into agreement with God and accept everything we do is for **HIS Kingdom**.

In the prior section, we discussed Romans 8:15 where the author Paul describes us as God's children, being adopted into sonship with our Father. But it doesn't stop there. We are further described to be *heirs* of God's glory in verses 16 and 17. *Brace yourself now. Meli is gonna school you some more. Forewarning: this book will have many, and I mean many, more lessons.*

The Merriam-Webster dictionary defines heir as *"a person legally entitled to the property or rank of another on that person's death."*[1] To understand it even deeper, I want to bring up the Messianic usage of the Greek origin word for heir, *klēronomos*. This word is defined as *"one who receives his allotted possession by right of sonship."*[2] Now... I hope you are still reading. I promise it'll be worth it.

Because God adopted us into His family, we have been saved for all eternity. *"For he has rescued us from the kingdom of darkness and transferred us into the Kingdom of his dear Son, who purchased our freedom and forgave our sins."* (Colossians 1:13-14 NLT).

We have rightful ownership to receive our Father's Kingdom in Heaven. Not only will we receive this inheritance after our life on Earth but we should view ourselves with rightful ownership to all that God has in store for us *while on this Earth.*

Now, I'm not trying to set up this concept that you should be asking God, *"Where's my throne? Where's my horse? Where's my prince charming?! God I'm an heir now so 'where it at doe'?!"* That type of attitude sounds a lot like the parable of the prodigal son in Luke 15:11-32. The son was asking his dad for an early inheritance because he was so consumed with material things. In the end he learned a valuable lesson, yet he was still loved unconditionally by his father no matter his mistakes. While it is comforting to know God will always accept us back, this story is not meant to be a license to do whatever we want.

What I want you to realize is that you have access to all you need and *will need* in the future to fulfill your calling for the glory of God. That's why it is so important to know **who's** kingdom you are building for. If you are building for your Heavenly Father, you will be guided by the Holy Spirit and provided for by God. But if you are building for yourself, then you better get ready to 'reap what you sow.' Building your own kingdom is not sustainable over a long period of time. At some point, you will fail without guidance from The Holy Spirit and could forfeit God's protection by being outside of His will.

I can't ignore the fact that Romans 8:17 says, *"...if we are to share in his glory, we must also share in his suffering."* Let me forewarn you, there will be discomfort in this journey. We will have trials. We will have tribulations. We will even have seasons of sufferings and heightened opposition along the way.

The only place that offers perfection is with Jesus in Heaven, so while we are here on Earth, we will always have hardship simply because we live in a broken world where sin runs rampant. But rest on God's word of comfort and protection in Psalm 91:14-15 NLT, *"The Lord says, 'I will rescue those who love me. I will protect those who trust in my name. When they call on me, I will answer; I will be with them in trouble. I will rescue and honor them.'"* We can rest assured that if we make the Lord our refuge, He will protect us and guide us along the way.

So don't fear the pains of this world, it's inevitable in our life. But find comfort knowing that our "Abba Father" desires to protect us. And we surely will be if we remain in His will and choose His Kingdom.

REFLECTION

- Think about and describe the importance of building for God's Kingdom instead of building your own.

- When have you seen God guide and provide for you when you've done something that honors Him? Compare a time when you pursued your own path, in an effort to honor yourself or others. Outline the specifics and reflect on the details.

- Write down your response and thoughts to Romans 8:17 "...*but if we are to share in his glory, we must also share in his suffering.*" What comes to your mind about sharing in God's glory? What about sharing in His suffering?

- Explain why it may be worth pursuing God's Kingdom even if we may endure suffering in our journey.

DEMOLISH MENTAL STRONGHOLDS

"The weapons we fight with are not the weapons of the world. On the contrary, they have divine power to demolish strongholds. We demolish arguments and every pretension that sets itself up against the knowledge of God, and we take captive every thought to make it obedient to Christ."

2 Corinthians 10:4-5 NIV

Unfortunately there are still many believers who are not operating in their lives with the confidence that they are adopted into sonship with God even through the redemption of Jesus Christ. I feel a big portion of that is because of the tactics of the enemy. Satan is a liar and attempts to set up strongholds in our mind. We can fall victim to the deceitful lies because we simply choose to believe them and/or we may not be aware of how to use God's mighty weapons to fight against it. As described in Joyce Meyer's book, *"Battlefield of The Mind"* she states, "A stronghold is an area in which we are held in bondage (or prison) due to a certain way of thinking."[1]

In another notable book, *"Killing Kryptonite: Destroy What Steals Your Strength"* written by John Bevere, uses the illustration and comparison of Superman and his weakness, kryptonite. His comparisons that we, as God's children, possess the supernatural power much like Superman, because we are supernaturally empowered by God through His Spirit. But what is this weakness that Superman has? Kryptonite. Bevere sets up the scene explaining, "Kryptonite's huge advantage over Superman is that it isn't easily recognizable, so he [Superman] could come under its effects prior to identifying it." [2]

The unrecognizable kryptonite that diminishes the power of Superman is similar to how the enemy's lies operate in our lives. Satan holds no authority since Jesus Christ does (see Matthew 28:18), so *'ol' boy* only can operate out of deception and accusation. But, unfortunately, many believers do not fight against the lies of the enemy and don't even recognize that he plants those thoughts in our mind. When we allow those thoughts to become instinctive to our behavior, that's when we know a stronghold has formed.

"For we are not fighting against flesh-and-blood enemies, but against evil rulers and authorities of the unseen world, against mighty powers in this dark world, and against evil spirits in the heavenly places." (Ephesians 6:12 NLT). Satan loves to play on our insecurities and weaknesses. He wants the condemning thoughts to cripple and paralyze us from doing the work of God or even abandon our faith all together. You may have heard thoughts similar to the following, "You're not good enough," "You can't make a difference," or "Why try when everything you do fails?" Satan is an accuser and he always seeks to tempt us, condemn us, shame us, and guilt us. Essentially his entire purpose is to kill, steal, and destroy, but the beautiful thing about Christ is that He stands in position to provide us with life, and life to the full (see John 10:10).

So how can we break down those mental strongholds like a wrecking ball? *Queue Miley Cyrus: Wrecking Ball* We demolish them! And lucky for us, *no Miley Cyrus needed to be able to do that.*

Just like Corinthians 10:5 says, satanic attacks and accusations that enter your mind must be *held captive* and *made* obedient to Christ. We demolish the lies and arguments by *"putting on the full armor of God"*. Now, this isn't *literal armor* like a medieval knight wears in battle. *Sorry to bust your bubble 'Game of Thrones' junkies.* But we have something more powerful even if it isn't *physically seen.*

"Therefore, put on every piece of God's armor so you will be able to resist the enemy in the time of evil. Then after the battle you will still be standing firm. Stand your ground, putting on the belt of truth and the body armor of God's righteousness. For shoes, put on the peace that comes from the Good News so that you will be fully prepared. In addition to all of these, hold up the shield of faith to stop the fiery arrows of the devil. Put on salvation as your helmet, and take the sword of the Spirit, which is the word of God."

Ephesians 6:13-17 NLT

These are God's mighty weapons given *freely* to His children: God's Word, prayer, hope, love, faith, and the Holy Spirit. They are all powerful and effective. This is why it is so vital as believers to constantly read God's Word and to be surrounded by other believers, empowered by the Holy Spirit, to walk alongside us in this journey. Our brothers and sisters that walk alongside with us, should point us back to God's Word rather than their own opinions or bias. If we don't know what God's Word says, how will we know the difference between Satan's lies and God's truth? We will discuss in the next section about studying God's Word.

Study God's Word

"*Women of the Word: How to Study the Bible with Both Our Hearts and Our Minds*" is written by Jen Wilkin. She summarizes true Bible study beautifully, "...sound Bible study transforms the heart by training the mind and it places God at the center of the story."[1]

This book breaks down how to study and comprehend the Word of God and the application of it in our lives. This style of studying the Word is known as an expository approach that is helpful with the application of Biblical principles. I am *so* grateful for my friend Jackie, who I mentioned earlier. She introduced me to this book and came alongside with me to study and interpret God's word. It was *life changing* to my faith. I grew leaps and bounds by having a firm foundation of scripture to deflect the enemy's lies in my life.

As I studied God's Word more, my passion and hunger for His Word and His desires grew with it. I truly understood what it meant to '*hunger and thirst for righteousness*' as described in Matthew 5:6. My identity grew firm in Jesus and my faith continued to grow. I began to truly understand the characteristics of our loving and sovereign Father.

The saddest thing I've discovered along my journey is that some people who proclaim the Word of God often times misinterpret and take scripture out of context. Because of Bible illiteracy, it can result in a lot of church hurt, division, skepticism, and people all together turning away from Christianity. I have heard *too many* people describe God from the Old Testament as an evil, angry, wrathful God. Although God did reveal His wrath after countless cycles of disobedience and idol worship, there's more to God than His judgment. God is just. God is merciful. God is grace. He isn't evil, but He also cannot *ignore sin* because He is Holy.

Some of the very characteristics of the Lord even in the Old Testament are stated this way, *"The Lord, the compassionate and gracious God, slow to anger, abounding in love and faithfulness, maintaining love to thousands, and forgiving wickedness, rebellion, and sin. Yet he does not leave the guilty unpunished; he punishes the children and their children for the sin of the parents to the third and fourth generation."* (Exodus 34:6-7 NIV).

God loved us *so* much, and knew our patterns of disobedience would keep us separated from Him, so his redemptive plan for humanity was to send Jesus Christ as an ultimate sacrifice for all of our sins (see John 3:16). What evil, angry, wrathful God would give us *so much* grace?

REFLECTION

- Write down your thoughts about your identity and your worth. Do they line up with what God's Word says about who you are in Christ? Identify points where your thoughts might be accusing thoughts planted by Satan.

- What thoughts come to your mind about pursuing the path that God intends for you? Does this invoke fear, anxiety, peace, joy?

- Do you currently study God's Word? If so, how has studying the Word helped you? If not, set a goal to begin studying God's Word.

  Tip: This can be done in a group setting such as a Bible study or individually through Bible study plans via app or book. After you begin studying God's Word, take note of what you are learning and how it is helping to fuel your faith.

CHOOSE TO RENEW YOUR MIND

> *"Don't copy the behavior and customs of this world, but let God transform you into a new person by changing the way you think. Then you will learn to know God's will for you, which is good and pleasing and perfect."*
>
> **Romans 12:2 NLT**

The final piece of assuring our goals are God-driven and not from selfish ambition is to make the conscious choice to renew our mind. Our thoughts have influence on the choices and paths that we decide to take. That's why majority of this chapter is based upon the mental process before the application of pursuing our goals.

Romans 12:2 says that God *will transform us*. And how is that? Through changing the way we think by the power of the Holy Spirit. In other translations of this scripture it is phrased as *"...be transformed by the renewing of your mind."* To renew your mind, is defined through the Greek origin word *anakainōsis* as, *"a renewal, renovation, complete change for the better."*[1]

How does renewing of the mind happen? What does it take for us to be transformed? It is the Holy Spirit's work in us when we *choose* to believe our true identity in Christ and commit to studying God's word with the deliberate act of meditation on divine things. *"I meditate on your precepts and consider your ways. I delight in your decrees; I will not neglect your word."* (Psalm 119:15-16 NIV).

I don't know if you're like me but when I hear the word meditate, I tend to think of some *"new age type of thing."* Where meditation is used to reach an *"inner chakra" or pairing rituals with sage or crystals.* Y'all, I am **definitely not** talking about those rituals because those practices are purely mystical and fall under witchcraft and idol worship.

But meditating on the Word of God purely means to *"ponder, contemplate, or to have deep consideration of."* You are making the conscious choice to turn your thoughts in a new direction, which is towards God. When you do, God's Spirit will continue to transform you and through that transformation process you will learn to know God's will for your life. *"...His good and pleasing and perfect will,"* as the scripture phrases it.

So when *will we know* His will for our lives? In the following chapters, we will utilize practical methods to allow God to guide us and direct us in the development and pursuit of our goals. There will be various opportunities that we can allow God to speak to us and help us to learn His intended will for our lives.

Are you ready Goal-Getters? One chapter down… one step closer to achieving our goals.

REFLECTION

- What area in your life is God leading you to choose His way vs. your own?

- Do you find yourself contemplating on scripture as you read it? Have you tried pausing and meditating on certain words the Holy Spirit leads you to? Take note of the words that 'stick out.' Reflect on it and ask God to reveal what significance the word has in your life. Take the time to do an in-depth word study by studying the original Hebrew/Greek word for further insight.

- What scriptures do you go to for comfort? Do they have a pattern in a particular area of your life i.e. trust, fear, anxiety, worry, etc.? If there is a pattern, reflect if there is an 'inner root issue' (as discussed earlier) that needs to be brought to God in prayer to receive healing and restoration from. Refer back to the beginning of Chapter 1 for reference.

Prayer

Heavenly Father, thank You so much for loving me and calling me your own. I thank You God for adopting me into Your family and saving me from being separated from Your Holy presence for eternity. Help me to be able to walk in the fullness of life that You intend for me to experience. Help me to realize areas in my life where I may need to confess sin and repent in order to receive Your forgiveness and healing. Help me to know my identity as Your child and an heir to Your eternal Kingdom.

Lord, I fully surrender any plans that I have to build my own kingdom and instead set goals that are motivated by building up Your Kingdom. Give me a heart that desires to do Your will. Help me to demolish evil strongholds that go against Your truth and help me renew my mind through meditating on Your Word. Guide me to the scriptures You would like for me to focus on. Bring to my remembrance the truth of who You are and the truth of Your Word during heavily oppressed times. I thank You in advance for the work that You will complete in my heart and in my mind.

In Jesus' name I pray.
Amen.

Chapter 2:

CALLED TO BEAR FRUIT

*"A good tree can't produce bad fruit,
and a bad tree can't produce good fruit.
A tree is identified by its fruit.
Figs are never gathered from thorn bushes,
and grapes are not picked from bramble bushes.
A good person produces good things
from the treasury of a good heart,
and an evil person produces evil things
from the treasury of an evil heart.
What you say flows from what is in your heart."*

Luke 6:43-45
NLT

CALLED TO BEAR FRUIT

We mentioned Superman, Miley Cyrus, Game of Thrones….and now *'we 'bout to'* talk about fruit. Who knew all of these topics could flow together when discussing the pursuit of being a Goal-Getter?!

After being confident that we have broken past self-ambitious cycles and truly intend to pursue God-driven goals, we need to know *what* we are called to produce which is *good fruit*. As Luke 6:44 says, *"a tree is identified by its fruit."* The Greek word for fruit used is *karpos*. In the Luke scripture, it is referring to the growth of literal fruit on a tree but in other scriptures such as Galatians 5:22 and Ephesians 5:9 it speaks figuratively meaning *"an effect, result, or that which originates or comes from something."*[1]

You might realize it takes time for a tree to bear fruit. You plant a seed in the ground, wait for it to sprout and grow into a tree, and then you wait *again* for the actual fruit to develop *on* the tree. My human nature wants to be like Kimberly Wilkins aka *"Sweet Brown"* and say, *"Ain't nobody got time fa that!"* But isn't that exactly what our world desires? Quick and instant results which often yield an even quicker end.

The world has embedded this mindset that if you hustle hard enough, you can obtain *anything and everything* on the time that you desire. Self-hustle has become the norm because of the adopted concept that if you do *more*, then you will produce *faster*. But the truth of the matter is that some things *will* take time and there is no self-hustle that can short cut the fruit that God wants you to develop.

Even when you look at smaller plants, such as flowers instead of trees, you will see that it still takes time to grow. A flower can sprout as quickly as five days after being planted yet won't bloom until six weeks later.[2] Now as far as planting a seed to grow a tree and bear fruit, it can take anywhere between six to ten **years** to fully harvest.

I'm so naturally inclined to take the 'easier route'. *Isn't it a temptation for us all*? To pick the quicker of the two options just to enjoy the benefit faster, but I challenge you to think about sustainability when comparing a flower to a fruit-bearing tree.

Regardless if someone is growing a flower or a tree, there is one thing that all plants have in common though. All plants need proper soil.

How is your soil?

> *"Still other seed fell on good soil, where it produced a crop- a hundred, sixty, or thirty times what was sown."*
>
> **Matthew 13:8 NIV**

Spoiler alert. I am not a farm girl. Or a girl with a "green thumb." *I mean*, if you know me personally, you can definitely tell I am *'all city.'* I've grown to enjoy nature and the peace that I feel while sitting in a quiet park but don't expect to see me camped out there too long. *I mean, these lashes and foundation just ain't made for the sun, ya know?*

I don't know too much about planting so the following will all be purely research and Holy Spirit-inspired so any plant enthusiasts reading this, *please* bear with me. Based on my research, I have learned properly developed and ready soil makes a difference in estimated growth time for flowers and fruit-bearing trees. Certain flower seeds need specific soil temperatures and need to be planted at a certain depth in order to properly grow. The same goes for fruit-bearing trees with the consideration of which season to plant due to the type of fruit you anticipate to grow.

This is exactly how the 'fruit' that we are called to bear works. The soil should be viewed as *our heart* and the seed sown should be viewed as the *Word of God*. 1 Peter 1:23 describes it as *"the incorruptible seed."*

Jesus actually breaks down a parable to his disciples and explains how the Word of God grows in each person's heart through different scenarios. I want to add commentary to each scripture to provide deeper reflection as we read each comparison.

PERSON 1

"Listen then to what the parable of the sower means: When anyone hears the message about the kingdom and does not understand it, the evil one comes and snatches away what was sown in their heart. This is the seed sown along the path."

Matthew 13:18-19 NIV

- You might acknowledge God because you desire to have hope but it's not a personal truth in your life.

- You can hear the Word of God and His promises but you don't truly *believe it* because of a hardened heart. The Word goes in one ear and out the other, making no impression or impact in your life.

- The enemy utilizes doubt in your mind, which can potentially develop spiritual strongholds.

PERSON 2

"The seed falling on rocky ground refers to someone who hears the word and at once receives it with joy. But since they have no root, they last only a short time. When trouble or persecution comes because of the word, they quickly fall away."

Matthew 12: 20-21 NIV

- You get excited after hearing a great message at church. You praise, shout, and rejoice in that moment. But you soon forget what you heard when the realities of life hit you. You unfortunately do not profit from what you heard.

- You have some level of faith but when something bad happens, you forget the excitement about the Word you had received. You allow discouragement and doubt to overtake you.

- You let your circumstances dictate the level of faith that you have.

PERSON 3

"The seed falling among the thorns refers to someone who hears the word, but the worries of this life and the deceitfulness of wealth choke the word, making it unfruitful."

Matthew 13:22 NIV

- You hear the word, it has an impression on you and takes root, but the demands of your career, home-life, responsibilities, etc., consume and entangle you—hindering you from growing in your faith in Jesus.

- Your desire for status and financial gain overrule your desire to know God. You still strive for selfish gain and the desire for wealth and success has deceived you. Your confidence is placed in wordly status and possessions which chokes the benefits of hearing God's Word.

PERSON 4

"But the seed falling on good soil refers to someone who hears the word and understands it. This is the one who produces a crop, yielding a hundred, sixty, or thirty times what was sown."

Matthew 13:23 NIV

- When you hear the Word of God you fully receive it and believe it by application of the Word in your life. You mediate on scripture and allow God to mold you according to His word.

- You have prepared to receive the Word through your daily discipline, action, and devotion to God.

- Because of your faith and obedience, you end up bearing fruit (crop) in abundance.

Obviously, our goal is to be Person 4. But where are you at right now? I truly believe we all have gone through (or will go through) the progression from Person 1 to Person 4. *I know that I have.* But I want you to review the reflection questions to think where you are currently and to be honest with yourself.

REFLECTION

- Have you ever planted something before? Were you satisfied with the results? What sort of preparation was involved in order to yield the best results? Take note of the process of physically planting to the comparative process to spiritual planting.

- In the list of Person 1 – Person 4, who would you best describe yourself as?

- How would you go about becoming Person 4 if you are not already?

PREPARE YOUR SOIL

"So neither the one who plants nor the one who waters is anything, but only God, who makes things grow."

1 Corinthians 3:7 NIV

Your upbringing and the things you experienced in your childhood may have a direct effect on the condition of your heart. It's unfortunate that many of us can look back at our childhood and reflect on some pretty damaging moments. So how do we prepare our heart (soil) to be like Person 4 in the last referenced section?

The three things that soil needs are: mulch, fertilizer, and organic matter. Much like believers, we need three key things as well: the Word, Worship, and Prayer.

Now, each word isn't a replacement for each physical item, nor have I listed them in any particular order. But each one is essential to cultivate and prepare our hearts.

WORD:

"For the word of God is alive and active. Sharper than any double-edged sword, it penetrates even to dividing soul and spirit, joints and marrow; it judges the thoughts and attitudes of the heart."

Hebrews 4:12 NIV

*"The grass withers, the flower fades,
But the word of our God stands forever."*

Isaiah 40:8 NKJV

Even if you were raised in a 'good home' and life was pretty easy, if you don't have any sort of exposure to the Word of God, you will see very little spiritual growth. Being exposed to God's Word can transform your mind *and* heart. It doesn't just help cultivate who you are, but it helps you grow in your trust to your 'Gardener,' who is God.

Worship:

"I will praise the Lord at all times. I will constantly speak his praises. I will boast only in the Lord; let all who are helpless take heart. Come, let us tell of the Lord's greatness; let us exalt his name together."

Psalms 34: 1-3 NLT

"Great is the Lord! He is most worthy of praise! He is to be feared above all gods. The gods of other nations are mere idols, but the Lord made the heavens!"

1 Chronicles 16:25-26 NLT

Singing songs in a church setting isn't the only time you can experience worship. Worship simply means: *"to have reverence (deep respect and honor) towards God."*[1] You can acknowledge how good God is during reflection, serving in ministry, tithing, prayer, *and* of course singing. Any expression of how good and amazing God is, is a form of worship.

Prayer:

"Then you will call on me and come and pray to me, and I will listen to you. You will seek me and find me when you seek me with all your heart."

Jeremiah 29:12-13 NIV

"Be joyful in hope, patient in affliction, faithful in prayer."

Romans 12:12 NIV

This is your communication with God. Prayer doesn't just mean a time when you make requests to Him but it's a time to truly connect with our Holy God. Open up to Him. Be vulnerable. Be honest. Listen to what He has to say. Allow your time of prayer to be an opportunity for meaningful conversation. (Refer to page 157 for a basic outline of the structure of prayer.)

As we recall, the three physical items needed to develop nutrient-rich soil were mulch, fertilizer, and organic matter. But we know one final thing that is missing that actually *grows* the seed in soil. That is water.

A seed cannot sprout, and a plant cannot thrive without it. Now from a believer standpoint, we know *who* our source of *living water* is, Jesus Christ. And without Him, there is no growth.

REFLECTION:

- Reflect on the condition of your heart (soil).

- How often do you utilize: the Word, Worship, and Prayer in your daily life? Are there ways you can improve each area? If so, how will you aim to begin doing so this week?

YOU CAN'T BEAR FRUIT WITHOUT JESUS

"Remain in me, as I also remain in you. No branch can bear fruit by itself; it must remain in the vine. Neither can you bear fruit unless you remain in me. I am the vine; you are the branches. If you remain in me and I in you, you will bear much fruit; apart from me you can do nothing."

John 15:4-5 NIV

Although this book will provide practical tools for determining and achieving your God-driven goals, we have to understand that we cannot truly bear fruit without our connection to Christ. How can a seed grow if there is no source of water to nourish it?

Jesus gave clear instruction in John 15:5 that if you remain connected to Him, you *will* bear much fruit. *Wow,* that is an amazing promise! If we think that we can truly receive the type of success that God wants for us, *without Him,* we are surely wrong. John Piper said it well when he said, *"If we are not united to the vine so that Christ's life is flowing into us, then his words, his love, his joy will be utterly and totally barren. Nothing of lasting value will come from us."* [1]

Further, John 15:16 NLT says, *"You didn't choose me. I chose you. I appointed you to go and produce lasting fruit, so that the Father will give you whatever you ask, using my name."* I want to remind us of the Greek word, *karpos*. As defined earlier in this chapter, it is *"a result, that which originates from something."*

If Jesus is telling us that we can't obtain particular results without abiding in Him, then it would lead us to believe that He is our 'something'. He is our source for life – *the Living Water.* So then we may ask the question, what does it mean to remain in Jesus?

The entire context of these passages is Jesus command to love people. In verse 17 it says, *"This is my command: Love each other."* Therefore, abiding in Jesus bears fruit, which one of the main fruits we can bear is loving others as Jesus loves us. It means letting the love, which we constantly receive from Christ as we abide [or remain] in him, flow through us and out to others for their benefit. [2]

As believers, we shouldn't do things for the pure benefit of ourselves or for our own selfish gain but rather to serve other people. When you think about a farmer growing a fruit tree, the fruit is picked off to provide benefit to others. But the fruit doesn't just benefit others in need of it, it also provides a source of food and income for the family growing it. When walking in purpose to love and benefit others, we too will be sustained and provided for as well.

Founder of the Confident Woman Company, Amanda Pittman, mentioned in an online teaching program *"Three Components of Your Calling"* that as followers of Christ we essentially all have the same purpose.

We are commanded to:

- Spread the gospel (see Mark 16:15).

- Make disciples (see Matthew 28:19).

- Obey His commandments (see John 14:15).

- Become like Christ (see 1 Peter 2:21).

- Walk in the specific calling predestined for us (see Ephesians 2:10).

Insert the wide-eyed shocked emoji *We are called to do all of that?!*

I know that sounds like *a lot* of pressure. But what should provide you comfort is that Jesus himself said, *"With man this is impossible, but not with God; all things are possible with God."* (Mark 10:27 NIV). If we are appointed to bear fruit and called to pursue our purpose with the above referenced commands, the *only way* to fulfill that is to remain connected and dependent upon Him.

Although we have the same purpose, the *avenue* or the specific *calling* for how we fulfill that purpose will be different. Just like there are various types of fruits, there are various roles and paths for the Kingdom of God.

Pittman phrased it this way, "Our life is a series of mini assignments. As you are faithful with each assignment, they will typically line up with a theme and unfold your calling before you." The development and achievement of your goals may develop a systematic theme. In a later chapter, we will discuss *"Goal Building Blocks"* which will help us interpret a potential theme or pattern towards our calling.

On page 160, you will find a reflection exercise to utilize for clarity on the avenue and/or calling for your life. I want to encourage you not to focus on *'figuring out'* your calling. It is not a requirement to pursue your purpose. Often times it will be revealed to you as you continue to *'press on'* towards your goals.

God desires an intimate relationship with us more than simply revealing the path He has ordained for us to walk. If He gave us the entire blueprint of our calling all at once, that would take away from our true dependency upon Him. And because dependency is such an important part of our relationship with Christ, you will notice the repeated theme in each section: determining your goals, good stewardship over them, and pursuing them, will all be linked to remaining dependent upon Him. When we walk in purpose, others will benefit from our obedience, but also know that we too will benefit.

There will be fulfillment, accomplishment, and most importantly growth. Allow Jesus to provide the essentials to your heart with His unfathomable love. And through that, we will bear fruit. *Good fruit.*

REFLECTION

- How does understanding your 'sole purpose' and commands as followers of Christ provide deeper insight to determining your goals?

- Can you think of people who have revealed *good fruit* and the impact that it has made on a community?

- How can this reflection inspire you to bear *good fruit* for the benefit of others? How could this benefit you (and your family)?

- What has God specifically called you to do? How does it align with His commands and your gifting? See page 160 for self-evaluation and guided prayer for the avenue/calling in your life.

Prayer

Jesus, thank You for choosing me. I am so grateful that You love me unconditionally. It is encouraging to know that You will provide all I need to fulfill my purpose as a follower of Christ. Help me to develop good fruit for the benefit of others. Help me to remain connected to You through the Word, worship, and prayer. Lord, help provide the desire to do You will and to serve others. Remind me that apart from You, I can do nothing and the only way to produce good fruit is through connection with You. Thank You that You take into consideration my interests, gifts, and roles in life when serving Your Kingdom through my specific calling. Help me to always remain dependent upon You in this journey.

In Jesus' name I pray.

Amen.

Chapter 3:

Determine Your Goal

"People may plan all kinds of things, but the Lord's will is going to be done."

Proverbs 19:21
GNT

DETERMINE YOUR GOAL

Yassss. We are at the stage of determining a goal! *Blow the confetti! Turn up the music! Queue the shoulder dancing! *Insert Michael Jordan lip poked out and shoulders bouncing side to side gif*

Okay, let's not get too excited since there will be a lot more work involved. But, if you're anything like me (*a little extra*) you can take a break to celebrate this next step.

There have been several memes circulating on social media that say things like: *"Sis! Speak it into existence," "Claim it!"* and *"I declare (this) will happen in the name of Jesus!"* But declaring things, like having six figures in your bank account overnight, simply doesn't work. *Trust me... if it did... hello shopping spree!*

Declaring provision without understanding there is process to achieve what we desire, keeps many believers in a stagnant and unfruitful season in life. The mindset to *only* believe in the spiritual aspect of God's ability to provide is only partial to receiving it. Someone could even argue that it may seem lazy and maybe even prideful to think we can sit back, believe that God is going to do it all for us, and not even 'lift a finger.'

I know many of us don't necessarily view provision from God as something arrogantly expected but we should know that speaking affirmations without effort is truly inefficient.

Now, the word 'affirmation' is a culturally used word and often used in the *'new age'* belief; but utilizing it from a Biblical perspective is simply coming into agreement with God's promises rather than believing the power that our own thoughts can manifest *whatever* we want. This is exactly why we have to understand our purpose, know the promises written in God's word, and interpret them properly.

My husband, filled with so much wisdom and clarity, phrased it this way, "Dreams can inspire but goals can change your life." Which is true. The desires in your heart and the things you dream about can inspire the direction of your goals. But if you don't actually set and determine a course for achieving your goals, then your dreams simply remain just that: dreams.

Psalm 27:4 NIV says, *"Take delight in the LORD, and he will give you the desires of your heart."* In previous chapters, we discussed the importance of checking our hearts and motives. So we should imply in this section, that our desires line up with God's desires and aren't reflective of just our own. In my own journey of faith, oftentimes when a desire gets planted into my heart or was already in my heart but resurfaced, I found it was usually God prompting me to pursue it further. This may be how you begin to determine specific goals based on the prompting of the Holy Spirit.

It's unfortunate that Psalm 27:4 is another misinterpreted scripture and often improperly used by many. The book of Psalms is a collection of written hymns and prayers that expresses the heart and soul of humanity. Psalms is written by several spirit-led men and throughout the book they are praising, worshipping, and even repenting to God. Psalm 27 was written by King David, who is also known as 'a man after God's own heart'. He wrote several psalms, some crying out to God in repentance and remorse and others in praise and adoration. Psalm 27 specifically is a collection of wisdom and encouragement about remaining in God's will.

I'd like to remind you that as you continue to deepen your relationship with Christ you will continue to change. And as you continue to change, your longing and desire to be in God's will, will also grow.

So then, what practical way can we turn our dreams and desires (which are God-driven) into goals? Utilize a practical method to determine those goals.

The 3 C's to Determining Your Goals

I use the phrase 'determine your goal' because the concept of determining something takes deliberate thought, pondering, and even analysis to establishing a goal. Because we are being Goal-Getters, through a Biblical perspective, we will utilize spiritual and practical methods hand-in-hand. During this stage we will be planning and developing our goals before the deliberate act of pursuing them. Essentially, this is where we will be laying the foundation.

A favorite author of mine, Alli Worthington used spiritual and practical tools in her book *"Breaking Busy."* She noted the five Bad B's of coping with stress and the five F's of decision making.[1] She inspired me with her use of same-letter acronyms, so I created a practical tool that was easy to remember and even fun to say.

So here we are, the three C's to 'Determining Yours Goals': *Commitment, Consistency, and Christ.*

Commitment

> *"Commit your works to the LORD,*
> *And your thoughts will be established."*
>
> **Proverbs 16:3 NKJV**

The first C is **Commitment**. You want to be sure you determine a goal that you have the *ability* to be committed to. Sometimes we get so excited about the end result that we set extremely difficult goals with no regard to our daily responsibilities.

I had a friend who was in such a rush to graduate and earn her college degree that she overloaded her schedule by taking eighteen credit hours while working full-time. She even enrolled full-time during the summer semester as well. Not only did she feel overwhelmed, frustrated, and stressed out, but it seemed she was unfruitful in her results.

We want to avoid overcommitment and, of course, being unfruitful. There will always be a sacrifice when taking on new responsibilities and pursuing our goals. We have to evaluate not just the goal we want to obtain but also factor in our current season of life and our daily responsibilities and roles.

Are you a wife? A mother? A single father? A caretaker of an elderly parent? Whatever role you are currently called to in life, you will need to evaluate the degree to which you have the ability to commit to a new responsibility in pursuit of your goal.

Determine Your Season

Another important function of *Commitment* is to consider the current season you are in. The most popular scripture when referring to seasons is Ecclesiastes 3:1-22 NLT:

> *"For everything there is a season,*
> *a time for every activity under heaven.*
> *A time to be born and a time to die.*
> *A time to plant and a time to harvest.*
> *A time to kill and a time to heal.*

A time to tear down and a time to build up.
A time to cry and a time to laugh.
A time to grieve and a time to dance.
A time to scatter stones and a time to gather stones.
A time to embrace and a time to turn away.
A time to search and a time to quit searching.
A time to keep and a time to throw away.
A time to tear and a time to mend.
A time to be quiet and a time to speak.
A time to love and a time to hate.
A time for war and a time for peace."

Poetic snap. Those scriptures just echo poetry night, doesn't it? The entire book of Ecclesiastes has some '*deep bars*', so if you're in need of some of *deep poetic scripture* then that's the book to check out.

Ecclesiastes describes several different seasons, but I wouldn't say that each season is literally going to be the category of the season that you will be in. What the scriptures do provide is a visual representation of the shifts and changes of each one.

As mentioned earlier, Amanda Pittman, referenced in "Three Component of Your Calling," reminds us that we want to steward our season well. We will discuss stewardship a little later but for now, that simply means to allow your season to help shape the direction of your goals. You want to work *with* your season, not against it so that you can work smart, not hard. *Or at least, let's say, not too hard.*

If you are called to a season of rest, you obviously shouldn't be building. Or if you are in a season of waiting, you obviously can't receive. I have gone through several seasons and I usually don't recognize the shift in each one until I'm actually going through it.

The truth is, God will have to be the one to determine and reveal the season you are in. It's not a requirement just simply an encouragement so that you don't become frustrated by trying to work *against* your season.

You may utilize the prayer outline exercise (on page 157) to ask for God's wisdom and clarity. James 1:5 NLT says, *"If you need wisdom, ask our generous God, and he will give it to you. He will not rebuke you for asking."* So I encourage you to simply ask and see what the Lord reveals to you.

COMMITMENT TO THE LORD

"When you make a promise to God, don't delay in following through, for God takes no pleasure in fools. Keep all the promises you make to him. It is better to say nothing than to make a promise and not keep it."

Ecclesiastes 5:4-5 NLT

We have addressed the practical view of *Commitment* so now let's discuss the spiritual side. The above referenced scripture is *yet again, some 'deep bars' from Ecclesiastes.*

When we decide to make a commitment to pursue our goals, we aren't just making a promise to ourselves but we are also making a promise to God. I thank God for having such amazing grace and mercy because I can't think of how many times I have tried to commit to something and have failed. There were even times when I just straight up changed my mind. *Can we say 'indecisive much'?*

I don't want you to read this scripture in Ecclesiastes and live in fear of experiencing shame or guilt should you commit to a goal, only to realize later that you can't fulfill it. But I want to encourage you to be intentional about your decision. We should take pursuing our goals seriously, because in the end, the application of these tools will help guide us and develop us more into God's specific calling on our lives.

Although we all have the same purpose as believers, we each will have a unique calling. Our desires, dreams, and even our gifts, talents, and abilities will be utilized in the pursuit of our goals.

REFLECTION

- What biblical affirmations do you meditate on to fuel your faith?

- How do these affirmations line up with God's promises? Where can this be found in scripture?

- What is a dream/desire of yours? How does this line up with scripture or God's commands as followers of Christ?

- What goal are you considering? Are you able to commit to it given the roles and responsibilities you are called to? How does it line up with the season of life you are in?

- Are you willing to make a full commitment to the Lord with pursuing this goal?

Consistency

"Therefore, my dear brothers and sisters, stand firm. Let nothing move you. Always give yourselves fully to the work of the Lord, because you know that your labor in the Lord is not in vain."

1 Corinthians 15:58 NIV

The second C is **Consistency**. The concept of being consistent is to develop rhythm, routine, and repetition. As we are in the planning and developing stage of our goals, we want to be sure that we can essentially *plan* a specific time to fulfill achieving our goal.

Consistency goes hand in hand with commitment as they will both be involved with answering the important questions, *"How can I fulfill this obligation?"* and *"What consistent routine can I implement to achieve this goal?"*

In the *Commitment* portion, you took into consideration your current roles, responsibilities and season. In this portion of *Consistency*, I want you to brainstorm the available time you can set aside to pursue your goal.

A very popular goal that people often have is to lose weight. You might ask, *"Now Meli, how does this line up with our purpose as a believer?"* Well, our physical health means a lot to God. Scripture often discusses the subject of glorifying God with our bodies, because it is the temple of the Holy Spirit (see 1 Corinthians 6:19-20) and taking care of the gifts He has given us, like our bodies, is a form of worship (see Romans 12:1).

The initial desire to lose weight might begin after self-criticism concerning our physical appearance, or maybe even something a little deeper, like a negative medical report about our health. But the next question is: *how* could you get from initial desire to actual application? Let's dig deeper to find out.

If you utilize the first C: *Commitment*, the following questions might be taken into consideration:

- Are you willing and able to commit to losing weight?
- What is your weight loss goal and when do you plan to obtain it?
- Are you in a season in life that would allow a consistent routine in the gym?
- Are you willing to commit to adjust your eating habits?
- Are you able to commit to the time to cook meals at home?
- Do you have a family that would be affected by trips to the gym or modifications to meals cooked?

The answers to your questions in the *Commitment* portion will pair together with the questions under the *Consistency* portion. A few sample questions for *Consistency* would be:

- What rhythm and routine would you develop with planning and coordinating healthy meals?
- What day(s) and time(s) could you consistently commit to exercise?
- How would your work schedule effect consistency in your routine?
- How would weekends or planned vacations effect your consistent routine of exercise and eating well?

I remember when I was in a very busy season in life. *Let me tell you, 'ya girl' was always 'TIDE' ('tired' with some **major** emphasis).* I had desires to pursue new goals but I knew I wouldn't be able to be c*ommitted* due to the season and responsibilities in life. I also wouldn't be able to be *consistent* since I knew I initially couldn't even *commit* to the idea.

If you brainstorm a goal that you are not able to commit to right now, I encourage you to write it down to revisit another time. We want to assure that we are utilizing our time wisely and not putting a lot of energy into goals that we are unable to pursue right now. I have done that with several of my goals and I was able to pursue them in a different season of life. If it is truly a God-driven goal, then God will provide the correct timing to make it happen.

In summary, just like 1 Corinthians 15:58 says, we are encouraged to *"give ourselves fully to the work of the Lord."* When we are fully committed, we will remain consistent as well. And we know that if we provide commitment and consistency, we can find comfort knowing that when our work is in full dedication to the Lord, it doesn't go in vain.

BE CONSISTENT WITH YOUR TIME WITH GOD

"Very early in the morning, while it was still dark, Jesus got up, left the house and went off to a solitary place, where he prayed."

Mark 1:35 NIV

Something that we should always be *Consistent* with is our personal time with the Lord. Throughout the Bible, many people sought the Lord *'very early in the morning'* because it gave them the opportunity to break free from distractions and truly allow them to *be still*.

In this modern age, where we have smart phones with notifications from *'every app under the sun'*, along with demanding schedules, we have to be very intentional about scheduling consistent time with the Lord. Seeking time with God very early in the morning might be a wise choice for some of us but not everyone is a morning person (well, *except me*). *You know that annoying coworker who strolls up to work full of energy and conversation first thing in the morning? Yeah... that's me!* But nonetheless, I want to encourage you to reflect and evaluate what time of the day works best for *you*.

Jesus made sure to have a consistent routine to remain connected, refilled, and refreshed with the Father. *I mean*, Jesus was casting out demons, healing 'folks' left and right, and constantly outpouring to those around Him, so He *'most definitely'* needed to be refreshed. Jesus was God in bodily form, but also flesh and blood. He *needed* focused and alone time with the Father.

Even if we don't compare our daily lives and routines to what Jesus did, we still serve a mighty purpose for the Kingdom and will need to be filled spiritually as well.

I'm a wife, a mother, and full-time employee. I have enough trouble having to balance dinner routines, serving in ministries and the community, work schedules, and keeping tidy (*which has gotten very low on my list now-a-days. God forbid somebody shows up unannounced!*). I also try to maintain a personal and spiritual life outside of my current responsibilities. I have found that in order to maintain consistent time with the Lord, I have to plan and schedule it into my life.

You cannot be passive about your alone time with God. Every time I did, I would inevitably let my day dictate *when* I could spend time with God and that left way too much room for excuses due to my lack of prioritizing.

I determined the best time for my alone time with God was early in the morning. I pair my alone time with God with my open line of communication with Him during the day, through constant prayer and acknowledgement of His presence. The key thing to my routine is that I make sure that I don't set a time limit on my alone time with God.

There might be a season in life where you are extremely busy and you might only be able to sit and be still with God during your lunch hour but I want to encourage you to try to schedule a consistent time where you won't have to rush your solitude with Him.

Something else to take into consideration is the question of how busy you really are. Are you overcommitted and/or overscheduled in your life? I encourage you to invite God into your situation to help you break free from things that might be a hindrance to your progression. I've been there before. But God gave me clarity and helped me break free by learning the importance of saying *'No'* and being honest with whomever I originally made a commitment to so that burden could be lifted off of my shoulders.

Reflection

- As you think about your goals, evaluate how you are able to remain consistent. Identify both roadblocks and consistent availability to pursue your goals.

- Describe your level of commitment to being consistent with the goals you determined to pursue.

- What rhythm or routine will you develop to remain consistent in achieving your goals?

- What current routine do you have with your alone time with God? If you do not have one, now is the time to determine a consistent routine and begin it this week.

CHRIST

"Work willingly at whatever you do, as though you were working for the Lord rather than for people."

Colossians 3:23 NLT

Now, the last C which is <u>the most important,</u> *of course, is* ***Christ***. We discussed how our underlying motivation for the pursuit of our goals should be for the purpose of God and not ourselves. We also discussed what our common purpose is and how we are called to bear good fruit. In this section, I want to provide some reminders and also key questions to reflect on. Below is a series of key questions to consider.

Does My Goal Line Up with God's Word?

- Is this goal, or even my motive behind the goal, going against the teaching and commands of God?
- Would this goal encourage anyone or myself to live a lifestyle displeasing to God?

If your goal does not line up with God's Word, then your goal needs to be omitted immediately. The path of being a Goal-Getter from a Biblical perspective **cannot** be pursued when it goes against God's Word.

For example: A goal to host an LGBT event glorifies their identity through their homosexuality and encourages same sex attraction.

To reshape your view and concept may be to help the LGBT community find their true identity in Christ. You may not necessarily be hosting the event to speak about their sexuality but if you find a passion for the mistreated LGBT community, it is first, to address the true inner root issue, which is their identity. Their identity as a person can be found in Jesus Christ, and Him alone.

Remember, we first identify as a Child of God. It is through the relationship with Jesus Christ that the Holy Spirit will transform the lives of ALL according to His purpose and will.

How Does My Goal Line Up with My Purpose as A Follower of Jesus?

Remember, this isn't just the unique *calling* or *avenue* but the purpose which we are called to serve the Kingdom by: spreading the gospel, making disciples, obeying His commandments, becoming like Christ, *and* walking in the specific calling predestined for us. Refer back to page 49.

Does This Goal Bring Me Closer in Relationship to Him or Further Away?

This one might be a little tricky. I remember in an extremely busy season, I was working two jobs, serving weekly on my church's student ministry as a group leader, attending a monthly serving meeting at the church, attending a monthly meeting with a nonprofit I volunteered for, and mentoring several people, all while being a wife and a mother.

There always seemed to be opportunities to do more. I felt if an opportunity came my way and God was glorified, that it was the right thing to do. Because of that flawed mindset, I quickly became overcommitted. I fell short in the primary roles God entrusted me with: 1st being His daughter, 2nd being a wife, and 3rd being a mother. Being a servant for others would come after true and proper stewardship of my first roles since God insists on a proper order.

I knew I had to evaluate my commitments when I had an opportunity to be a part of a 'higher-level' leadership training at my church. It would be a series of four weeks, meeting with my student pastor who would invest in us and join us in additional studies. Immediately when I got offered this opportunity, I broke down crying. *You can say, I was 'over the limit' and 'over capacity.'* I couldn't imagine putting something else on my plate. Not only did I feel pressure from the potential burden of accepting, but a lot of feelings of guilt resurfaced from the realization of how much time I've spent away from my family serving other people.

It never dawned on me, that I hadn't submitted my opportunities to serve in the church or volunteer for nonprofits to God. I should have *always* asked for His wisdom and direction, instead of *'leaning on my own understanding'*.

Proverbs 3:5-6 NIV gives some useful advice in doing just that, *"Trust in the Lord with all your heart and lean not on your own understanding; in all your ways submit to him, and he will make your paths straight."*

Just because it was a *good thing* to do, didn't mean that God was necessarily calling me to it. When I realized that I never asked God before accepting or denying certain opportunities, I took the time to ask the Lord about the leadership training at the church. I asked God, *"Lord, is this something that you want me to commit to?"* God's response to me was, *"Will this bring you closer to me or farther away?"*

I realized that I was committing to doing so much *for* God that I was pushing away time *with* God. I realized that it was something that would bring me farther from Him. He confirmed with me not to accept this opportunity since my heart's true desire was to keep Him first along with the proper order as being a wife and mother before serving others.

I encourage you to really ponder if the pursuit of any particular goal would take away from your *consistent* time with God. Again, we may have seasons that are naturally busier than others, (having a new baby, caring for a hurt or sick family member, kid's extracurricular activities, whatever it might be), but we need to be assured the goal that we desire to pursue won't hinder our intimacy with God. Remember, good fruit is only truly developed by abiding in Jesus Christ.

Colossians 3:23 calls us, *"To work willingly as unto the Lord rather than people."* Always remember that in our service to people we should be as fully committed to serving them as we are Jesus Christ. There is a misconception that only the most passionate followers of Christ would work in the church or other ministries, but God called all of us to be workers in all areas of life. We have been gifted with different skills and abilities, along with our own individual interests and passions. All of these can be utilized for the glory of God no matter what stage of life we are in.

If you desire to be a social media influencer, be sure the motivation isn't to receive validation and approval from others (as we discussed in Chapter 1.) But instead, *giving* to others, which can possibly be through impacting people for Kingdom's glory, exemplifying the teachings of Jesus, utilizing opportunities to share the Word of God to those who are lost, and/or essentially loving people as Christ loves us.

There are passionate believers who are real estate agents, bankers, teachers, social media influencers, personal trainers, students…the list goes on and on. The goal we wish to pursue doesn't have to launch into entrepreneurship or change your entire career path but these desired goals might lead and assist you to walk into your specific calling in life.

Even if the goal you wish to pursue is something you view as unknown territory, be encouraged to know since you have worked through each section of this book, that God may be redirecting your path to one He intended for you all along.

REFLECTION

- After reviewing the key questions under the *Christ* portion of this book, are your goals worth pursuing?

- How do your goals draw you to full dependency on Christ or how do they push you further away? Determine if there are adjustments to be made, if this goal will be utilized in a different season/stage of life, or if it needs to be omitted altogether.

- How can you work willingly as unto the Lord in your current career? If you are a student or stay at home parent, how can you do the same?

Prayer

Lord I am so grateful that I can utilize practical tools and wisdom to determine if the goals I wish to pursue are in alignment with Your will. I fully commit my work to You Lord and ask that You can help establish my thoughts and the path You have ordained for me. Help me to be fully committed to You, consistent with our time together, and assure the goals I pursue line up with Your Word. Help me when I fall short and get distracted from pursuing my purpose. Help me to realize that seeking You first should be the most important step when it comes to doing Your will. I thank You God that my work does not go in vain when it is fully committed to You Lord.

In Jesus' name I pray.
Amen.

Chapter 4:

BE A GOOD STEWARD OF YOUR GOAL

*"If you are faithful in little things,
you will be faithful in large ones.
But if you are dishonest in little things,
you won't be honest with greater responsibilities."*

Luke 16:10
NLT

BE A GOOD STEWARD OF YOUR GOAL

By now, we have planned and coordinated our God-driven goals to assure we can fully commit, be consistent, and that the goal itself is in alignment with God's commands. You would naturally think the next step is to begin the pursuit to achieving those goals... *Nah*. Sorry to disappoint you. We need to add some meat to those bones. *Well, if you're vegan, we'll say add some kale to those potatoes...or somethin' like that. Hey, Meli's trying to be sensitive to all parties here!*

In each section we will discuss the importance of being a good steward of our goals. Merriam-Webster defines *steward* as *"one who manages direct affairs"*[1] and *stewardship* is *"the act of conducting, supervising, or managing something."*[2] The way to be a good steward of our goals is to essentially be a responsible manager of them.

The very first job that I had was at Subway. I was a *Sandwich Artist. Ooo so fancy, huh?* I did so well as a Sandwich Artist that I became a shift manager. I held the responsibility of opening, balancing registers, prep and setup of stations, delegation of tasks, and overview of staff to assure smooth operations. Holding the position as a manager, I understood that there were things under my direct supervision. It was my job to assure things operated properly under my care. One way I assured good stewardship was through proper planning and coordinating.

PLAN ACCORDINGLY

> *"Good planning and hard work lead to prosperity,*
> *but hasty shortcuts lead to poverty."*
>
> **Proverbs 21:5 NLT**

Unlike planning the initial blueprint of our goals, this section will utilize the application of pursuing our goals and devising plans needed to fulfill them. Have you heard of the famous quote, "When you fail to plan, you plan to fail"? Did you know Benjamin Franklin is credited to have said this? *I'm wondering if you're just as shocked as I was? Well, I guess he must know a thing or two to be the represented face of the $100 bill.* I essentially think about that quote after reading Proverbs 21:5.

The book of Proverbs has some amazing 'life lessons' and words of wisdom to live by. Good planning paired with hard work gives us the imagery of prosperity, wealth, success, and abundance. Yet the opposite, 'hasty shortcuts' makes you think of lack of, poverty, and deficit.

Back in 2018, the Lord put a desire in my heart to learn more about fasting. As we discussed in the previous chapter, often-times God will place a desire in your heart that nudges you to pursue it further. That's what happened in my case. Fasting was unknown to me and I was ignorant to the significance of denying our flesh. I learned more through listening to several sermons and practicing fasting more frequently in my life. Later in the year, the Lord increased my desire to not only fast individually but to provide an opportunity to educate others and fast along with me.

That was how the development of one of my goals, to host a monthly fasting meeting, began. Although, this goal was developed near the end of 2018 it wasn't until 2019 when I was able to fully launch and go forth with pursuing. I utilized the three C's of 'Determining Your Goal' to determine my ability to *commit*, my required *consistency* to this commitment, and assure this goal glorified *Christ* and lined up with His word.

In order to actively pursue my goal, it required intentional planning, research, and outlining. I had to brainstorm the title of the meeting, where it would be held, how many times we would meet, the length of each meeting, what would be discussed, whether I would need other people to help me host it, etc. Of course, alongside with my own individual responsibility to plan and research, I was constantly praying and asking the Lord for continued guidance and direction. *"A person's steps are directed by the Lord. How then can anyone understand their own way?"* (Proverbs 20:24 NIV).

Not only did the Lord provide guidance and direction, but the Holy Spirit would provide me with inspired thoughts. I was relying on the wisdom from God along with my effort to take notes, pray over, and reflect on often.

When I determined the structure of the meeting, I developed the blueprint. Even though I had the initial structure and blueprint, once I began to pursue my goal and host my meeting it still required proper planning during my pursuit. Think of the construction of a home, the contractor will have the blueprint of how the house is to look upon completion. Yet, the contractor still needs to properly plan during the building process in order to be efficient and complete the job by a particular date.

We should be properly prepared before *and* during the active pursuit of our goals. Do not take this lightly. It's important to work with excellence and to pair hard work ethic with our faith. Not only does this represent His Kingdom well, it will help us achieve our goals timely and efficiently.

REMOVE DISTRACTIONS

"Therefore, since we are surrounded by such a huge crowd of witnesses to the life of faith, let us strip off every weight that slows us down, especially the sin that so easily trips us up. And let us run

with endurance the race God has set before us."

Hebrews 12:1 NLT

*A*hh. Distractions. *"A thing that prevents someone from giving full attention to something else."*[1] We can fall victim to being consumed with daily distractions and not even realize that we are choosing something of *lesser* importance over something of *higher* value. *I know I've been guilty of it.* I think back to how often I choose to scroll on social media rather than create memories with my daughter or even engage in a thoughtful conversation with my husband.

Now, distractions are things we *choose* to spend our time with. Social media isn't *a person* that can just walk into the room while we are spending time with our family and take our attention away from them. We intentionally *choose* to click on our apps and feed the temporal feeling of, what is essentially a perverted desire to connect with people, through our phone screens. That's a whole *'nother subject to discuss in a whole 'nother book. But I know what you're thinking. Come on Meli. It's 2019.* I'm not implying that we shouldn't *ever* get on social media, I just want you to be cautious about how you spend your time, what you are choosing to spend your time with, and how those 'things' (distractions) could possibly hold you back from achieving your goals.

We must be willing to remove and separate from anything that *slows* us down. The author of Hebrews describes it as "...*stripping off every weight... especially sin that easily trips us up."* Now, people tend to get really uptight when the word *sin* is used. But sin defined in the original Greek is *"an offence, violation against God and His law- whether in act or in thought, and/or miss the mark."*[2]

When you look at sin as anything that sets you 'off course' from the Will of God, it makes you realize there are a lot of things we should not allow to be a stumbling block in our life. Now, Social Media isn't a *sin* in itself, (even though my husband straight up calls it *'the devil'*!) I simply encourage you to evaluate how distractions can prompt a negative domino effect in your life and take your eyes off of Jesus. In our Christian walk, we have the responsibility to remove anything that endangers our relationship with Christ. If we set our eyes and focus off Jesus, that is how we stumble, lose focus, and possibly get entangled in sin through gratifying our flesh.

You may not be distracted by social media, maybe your distraction is Netflix. Whatever it might be, evaluate if you are engaging in activities, considered to be distractions, which would essentially delay achieving your God-driven goals. Find the balance between working hard and enjoyment. Be mindful of what you are truly receiving from engaging in an activity. Is it life giving? Will it help you be refreshed in pursuing your goals? Is it adding to your spiritual growth in Christ?

If you are choosing too much time on distractive activities then, *'strip it off.'* And *y'all, I mean in the Biblical sense.* Let go of the things that are holding us back from becoming Goal-Getters for the Kingdom of God.

REMOVE IDOLS

"Dear children, keep yourselves from idols."

1 John 5:21 NIV

Often when we hear the word 'idol' we think of stories in the Old Testament where they were building statues made of gold and shaping them into things like a calf but the modern day idol is much more dangerous because it's less obvious. An idol defined from the Hebrew origin word, *'eliyl*, means, *"of nothing, empty, vain, i.e. vain comforters."*[1] How often have we sought *empty and vain comfort* from 'things' rather than God?

I struggled with seeking validation and affirmation through the attention on social media. I knew that if I was having a bad day or didn't *feel* attractive that I could post a selfie and feel affirmed from the likes, comments, heart eye emojis, and even my girls *'gassing me up'* with the *"Yasss Boo I See You!"* comments. *Yeah,* it's not a golden calf but it was still something I turned to receive false comfort from rather than receiving true validation from God.

In the NLT translation, First John 5:21 says, *"Dear children, keep away from anything that might take God's place in your hearts."* Your idol could very well be the same that mine was, validation through social meal. Or maybe it could be an excessive escape to exercise and using the feeling of the endorphins to provide you with comfort. Or possibly a toxic relationship where you have become so addicted and dependent upon this person rather than dependent upon God.

Since we can fall so easily into the trap to put 'something' above our Father, I encourage you to bring this to God in prayer and ask Him to reveal anything in your life that you may be setting up as an idol. We want to keep Him in His Sovereign and rightful place at all times.

SET BOUNDARIES

When I hear the word 'boundaries,' I always think of a sermon that Sarah Jake Roberts preached when she said, *"...My edges was flourishing, my skin was smooth, my waist was snatched, because 'ya girl' messed around and got some boundaries!"* First of all, give me a dose of that and make it an extra-large, okay?!

Even though I wish boundaries could magically do that, she explained that her life was at its healthiest when she set determined boundaries and chose to live God's way as a standard for her life. I'm going to use this portion of the chapter to explain some healthy boundaries between a professional standpoint and a personal one.

PROFESSIONAL BOUNDARY

I currently work in corporate banking and the department that I work for handles commercial loan documents. Our department has separate specialized functions, but essentially everything flows from, back to, and all the way around to us again which basically means that we have *a lot* of responsibility. The bank I currently work for previously 'bought out' the bank where I was originally hired. And if you know anything about banking, you know that bank mergers can happen just as much as Cardi B uses the word "Okuurt." *Which is a lot y'all. Okurt?*

Because of so many buy-outs and mergers, the volume became much larger than the staff that we had on hand. Due to my workload, the only way to complete most of my tasks in one day was for me to skip lunches, stay late, and essentially not get up from my desk for water or even bathroom breaks. *Yeah.* None of that was healthy *at all.* I wasn't just mentally exhausted, but physically and emotionally, too.

I found myself always feeling stressed, weighed down, frustrated, and oftentimes crying in the bathroom praying for God to help me get through my day.

I would come home complaining with zero motivation to tend to the responsibilities or stewardship of being a wife and mother. I knew that I had to change something because the way my job affected me wasn't just during work hours, my family felt the effect at home, too.

God was always my source of comfort and would keep speaking to me the word, *'boundaries'*. Realizing that He was giving me the tools to endure in that season, I had to set up specific rules which would be viewed as a defined boundary. I refused to skip lunch, only stay thirty minutes past my shift time if needed and take water and bathroom breaks.

Because I set boundaries at work, does that mean I would no longer be working hard? *No.* Does it mean I need to have a bad and resentful attitude towards my managers? *Not at all.* I set up boundaries to assure I wasn't exhausting all of my energy at work, a situation that left me depleted and unable to be the wife and mother that God called me to be.

Remember how I told you in Chapter 1, that I wore the badge of honor as being a *workaholic? Well, not anymore.* That badge had been removed and I vowed to never pick it back up again. Which has provided me more peace and mental stability than ever before.

If you are experiencing a similar situation at your job, I encourage you to ask the Lord what clear and defined boundaries you may need to set up at your work place. Remember, setting a professional boundary is not an excuse to be resentful or *petty*. Still work as unto the Lord just within the perimeter of your job responsibilities and appropriate defined boundaries.

PERSONAL BOUNDARIES

Personal boundaries are going to be just as important as professional boundaries. Even if you're not in a high-stress work environment, you should still be mindful of your personal relationships and evaluate if there is a need for defined boundaries.

I'm a constant encourager, or an *empath* as some people describe it. I know a part of my specific calling is to **m**otivate, **e**ncourage, **l**ove and **i**nspire people (*which is why my nickname **Meli** is so special to me*). Since I am constantly outpouring to people, I have to be mindful of how full I am spiritually. If I have not allowed proper time with my Heavenly Father to allow His love to fill me up, so much so where I am overflowing, then it can be difficult to 'pour out' to others if there isn't much 'to give.' Of course, I'm just giving a metaphoric expression because regardless if we have spent one minute or one hour with the Father, the Holy Spirit may still prompt you to speak encouragement and life to a fellow brother or sister in Christ. But I encourage you to be mindful of the season you are in, the time and ability you have to be filled spiritually through intimate commune with the Lord, and how much you are pouring out to others.

If you are an encourager like me, you might find yourself having people constantly asking for your advice and needing to be uplifted. I advise you to set an appropriate boundary with your time. Now, there may come a time when someone may require an urgent need at 'the exact moment' but often, it's wise to set up a boundary during your available time. You want to honor your time with your family and any specific responsibilities such as being a good steward of your job during work hours. If I have a friend who is going through a divorce and needs sound advice, encouragement, and prayer, I may take a break and speak to her at that exact moment. But then, I may continue the conversation after work. The reality is that some people may not honor your personal time by becoming defensive, causing you to feel guilty, if you are unable to speak to them immediately. I advise you to set up clear distinct boundaries on your communication with them.

I never turn down a cry for help, but I will do my best to not neglect my family or put my job at risk. As I encourage people, I try to provide them with 'tools' to be able to receive strength, encouragement, and hope through their own developed relationship with God because I shouldn't be viewed as the redeemer, only Jesus Christ should be!

Because you are intending to pursue God-driven goals which may lead you further into your calling, the enemy will most likely try to distract you in various ways. A possible way is by attacking those around you who would seek your help and encouragement. You could potentially be utilizing your time ministering to everyone around you and becoming distracted from your key focus on pursuing your God-driven goal. Even if you are helping other believers, they could be swayed under Satan's influence to potentially delay, distract, or even cause you to forfeit pursuing your God-driven goals. Think of Peter when Jesus was telling the disciples that He would be dying on the cross.

> *"Peter took him aside and began to rebuke him. 'Never, Lord!' he said. 'This shall never happen to you!' Jesus turned and said to Peter, 'Get behind me, Satan! You are a stumbling block to me; you do not have in mind the concerns of God, but merely human concerns.'"*

Matthew 16:22-23 NIV

Peter was one of Jesus disciples, yet he operated in his own wisdom by trying to deter Jesus from going to the cross. Yet, what Peter was in agreement with was outside of the Will of God and Jesus assignment from the Father. It wasn't that Peter was *actually* Satan, but he was unknowingly being used to try to push an agenda to disrupt God's intended plan. But as we all know, *that didn't work* because God is all powerful and all knowing. Nothing can thwart the plans of our Almighty God.

I don't want you to neglect helping people, simply utilize prayer along with wisdom and discernment on the urgency of someone's need. Be sure to always point them to the True One, Jesus, who should always be their source of comfort and encouragement.

UTILIZE BOUNDARIES LIKE JESUS DID

"But despite Jesus' instructions, the report of his power spread even faster, and vast crowds came to hear him preach and to be healed of their diseases. But Jesus often withdrew to the wilderness for prayer."

Luke 5:15-16 NLT

I offer a final piece of advice on boundaries because I feel it is so important to assure we are not overexerting ourselves in areas holding us back from truly pursuing and achieving our goals. I want you to think about how Jesus had several opportunities to *over invest* in one area of His life than another.

Jesus was healing people left and right, ministering to groups and crowds, going from city to city spreading the Gospel, teaching and shepherding disciples, all while knowing He had to fulfill the ultimate calling in His life- dying on the cross as the ultimate sacrifice for humanity. If anyone should have felt stressed, overwhelmed, and overworked *surely* it would have been Him. Although Jesus wasn't married, had children, or clock in and out at a 9-5 job, He still set an example during His time on Earth for our modern day and age.

In Luke chapter 5 verses 12-16, we find Jesus in one of the villages where a man with severe leprosy was begging to be healed. Jesus healed this man but told him not to tell anyone, simply to let the priest examine him and make a sacrifice at the temple. But we read verse 15 that *someone may not have kept their mouth shut* because pretty soon, *'errybody and they mama' knew.*

But how did Jesus respond? He withdrew to solitude. Jesus didn't complain, rebuke the person He just healed, or even rebuke the crowds and tell them, *"Are y'all serious? Can you just give me a break for once?!"*

I don't know what would be more interesting to read about, Jesus actually responding how I do when I'm overwhelmed with stress or picturing Him using the Southern word 'y'all.'

Although there are several examples of Jesus setting up boundaries, the biggest one that I reflect on is his wise choice to withdraw and get in solitude with the Father. On our journey of stewarding our goals well, we want to make sure that we are mindful of our boundaries with work and people to assure what God is pouring into us is being poured out in appropriate areas during the proper time.

SHARE WITH DISCRETION

"When I was a child, I spoke and thought and reasoned as a child. But when I grew up, I put away childish things."

1 Corinthians 13:11 NLT

You want to be mindful with who you are sharing your ideas and goals with. There are people who are intended to be in our life that will assist us to get us closer to our calling, but everyone is *not* on our side. *Heck, think of Judas.* Now, I'm not trying to make you skeptical and lack trust in *everyone,* but I do want to encourage you to be mindful about oversharing. *Seriously, y'all...* not everyone on Facebook needs to know *every. single. detail.* I'm not saying that just as an annoyed Facebook scroller (*well, maybe I am... just kidding)* but I'm saying this more for the protection of your initial plans. Your *infant* goals and ideas.

Early in my walk of faith, I felt a deep desire in my heart to serve God. I wanted to have a direct impact in my community and work every single day with purpose. I was a Credit Analyst at the time and did underwriting for commercial lenders. I didn't feel much fulfillment during the five years that I was in that role. I knew in my heart I was called to something greater.

I felt that working with purpose meant to work for a non-profit or a ministry that served the community. So my initial thought was to get a job in that sector. A few months after this desire was stirring in my heart, our community bank announces they were getting bought out by a larger bank. As mentioned in the boundaries section, bank mergers happen quite a bit and through those mergers, the new company typically restructures roles and will often eliminate many positions.

So, the new company tells me that I will be losing my job at the end of transition. Of course I felt shocked, a bit hurt from not wanting to be kept with the company, but ultimately I received so much peace from God because I felt He answered my prayer about removing me from my current job to work at another job with purpose.

During that time, a lot of coworkers avoided me because they felt bad. There were others who sympathized with me and would ask what my plans were. I felt so much peace about what was going on, I would openly share about my relationship with God and express how I felt called to non-profit work. Yet, time went by and every avenue of interest in non-profit simply didn't happen. Our transition wouldn't occur for another six months after the notice of my terminated position, but during the pursuit of my next career, I began to feel lost in the route of my next career.

I wanted desperately to work for God and make an impact, but I began to question if non-profit was truly my path. I was left in an odd place trying to figure out the direction God wanted me in and wavering with my career choices like a seesaw. I wrestled with the idea and began to accept remaining in corporate. I knew I wanted a new position since I had grown so complacent in my current role.

Months continue to go by, four specifically, and people were leaving left and right. Two out of the three employees, who were selected to remain in my department, end up leaving and getting new opportunities before the merger was official. A few managers told me that executive management would reach out to me about an internal position since there were several open from people leaving the company. Even though, executive management would discuss a potential career opportunity with me, I was still questioned by several other managers about whether or not my career would be long-term or if I had plans to leave and work for a non-profit.

Mind you... I didn't tell *everyone* about seeking to work in non-profit work. So, it *had to have been* word of mouth from the people I *did* tell. In the end, I still was offered another opportunity in the company, but it was something brought up and questioned *several times*.

The feeling that I thought I would be called to non-profit truly was stemmed from the desire to serve. I was under the impression to live for God and work for His purpose was to work full-time at a church, ministry, or non-profit. The confusion was simply because I was still a 'babe' in my faith. *"When I was a child, I spoke and thought and reasoned as a child. But when I grew up, I put away childish things."* (1 Corinthians 13:11 NLT).

As I have grown in my faith so have my visions, goals, and direction. The path of my goals has become more clear and concise and each achieved goal seems to serve as a building block for even larger goals (which we will discuss in a later chapter).

I'll never forget when I was listening to a sermon series called "Marked: Approved in Private" from Transformation Church. Pastor Michael Todd said, "The easiest time to kill something is when it's in its infant stage." He talked about the key importance of discretion and not publicly letting everyone know what God is telling you in private.

Even though sharing how I thought I was called to a career in non-profit wasn't necessarily a developed *goal*, but rather a career choice, it still wasn't utilizing discretion at all. God was so patient with me through that stage of life though. He understood my heart when I was sharing the stories with my coworkers. He placed the desire to serve in my heart, but I still had to grow in maturity to truly comprehend that desire. Although it didn't hinder the job opportunity to where I am at now, it was a lesson to learn about the concept of only sharing with a select few.

I know it's tempting to share your dreams, visions, and goals with social media, but it can be a dangerous thing. For my situation, I was wavering so much with what I felt God placed in my heart, I could have added a lot of confusion to people who might view my own personal confusion as God being unclear and confusing. Not only could it hinder someone's relationship with God, but it could also discourage the clear path that God confirmed with you privately.

People could begin to sway you in a direction that God is not leading you to or even question your path because they don't understand it. So use discretion with sharing your goals with people and allow God to develop them in private. Allow your desires to grow, your vision to become more clear, and your faith to become more mature during this journey.

SEEK WISE COUNSEL

*"Plans fail for lack of counsel,
but with many advisers they succeed."*

Proverbs 15:22 NIV

In the previous section, we talked about the importance of discretion. But there's also significance in having wise counsel in your life. *I don't know if you're like me* but the phrase 'wise counsel' sort of makes me imagine a room with a long table, a group of stiffy *old folks* sitting around, waiting to brutally critique my plans and goals. *Ugh. How intimidating would that be*? But good for us, that's not at all what I mean by wise counsel.

As you should know by now, I'm gonna explain yet another definition. But I hope you can admit, you never thought a dictionary could provide so much insight! Now, the definition of counsel simply means, *'advice, guidance, and direction.'*[1]

It's smart to have people in our lives that can be a sounding board and provide us with guidance. I would say it's similar to having a support system but the flaw in simply having support *without guidance* is that support alone doesn't provide you with real growth. Having spiritually mature friends and mentors in your life, whom love and honor God and are willing to provide you with godly insight (even if it's something you don't want to hear) can be very beneficial.

"Wounds from a sincere friend are better than many kisses from an enemy." (Proverbs 27:6 NLT). *That's right,* sometimes people who are speaking truth and love can hurt us and it is our *'haters'* who can be smiling and fake applauding all while watching us walk down a destructive path. Since we had a discussion on discretion, you have to utilize wisdom and discernment on who you will allow to provide insight into your goals. And if you don't know what the word discernment means, I would describe it as *'having a deep intuition about someone or judging well'*.

In Christianity discernment is viewed as a spiritual gifting however the context of scripture (1 Corinthians 12:10) is specifically talking about the spiritual side of discernment by discerning spirits and against false prophets. Although that's an amazing gifting to have, I'm referring more to the *natural world* in utilizing good character of judgement.

What should you look for when it comes to having wise counsel in your life? One thing is, the person should be rooted in the Word of God. I'm not saying you need to quiz them and ask them, *"What year did Jesus first begin His ministry?! *Buzzer Sound* Wrong. Next!" Because seriously… Lezzz be real.* They don't need to be able to spit out Bible wisdom at the sound of a buzzer, but they should have a fair level of knowledge of scripture along with interpretation of it.

If you don't have a close friend that is rooted in God's word, possibly look into joining a Bible study, a church small group, or simply meet with the pastor at your church to seek direction and guidance. Be sure to continuously pray and ask God for wisdom, clarity, and direction to be sure you are led to the right people.

Another thing you should ask yourself is, "*What sort of fruit do they bear in their life?*" As we mentioned in Chapter 2, God intends for us to bear good fruit which is simply evaluating the kind of results this person yields in their life.

When I went on a journey to find '*my group,*' I was searching high and low. I joined a church small group, served on several ministries, and would even reach out to a few social media friends who I saw posting a lot of scripture and other Christian memes. I could have accepted *any* friendship that had *a sprinkle of Jesus in there* but because of discernment, I always sensed when it wasn't the best 'fit.'

I remember when I thought I found 'my girls' since we were doing devotionals together on the Bible app and seemed to have the same interests. But once we hung out, they engaged in a lot of gossip, judgment of others, and controversial topics which ended up grieving my spirit more than feeding it. *"Do not be misled: "Bad company corrupts good character"* 1 Corinthians 15:33 NIV.

During that season in life, God intentionally had me in insolation. I kept pursuing a community, but I never received what I was looking for. That desire to be fed spiritually needed to be first met by my Savior before I depended on anyone else. I admit there was still a lot of pleading, crying, and even frustration with God during that season of isolation. But now I can appreciate His desire for me to fully and entirely trust Him first because I could have possibly utilized people as my foundation rather than allowing Him to be *my firm foundation.*

God sent wise counsel as I grew and matured in my faith and I can now see how His timing was perfect.

Your wise counsel should be a support for you but also be willing to challenge you with guidance and direction. This group should help you think on the eternal things of God and contribute to your spiritual growth – *even if it's hard to hear*. Make sure they are rooted in God's Word and show results of good fruit. Then you will get to see the true representation of Proverbs 27:17 NLT, *"As iron sharpens iron, so a friend sharpens a friend."*

Goal-getters, be sure to let them sharpen you, not dull you.

Reflection

From each section in 'Be A Good Steward of Your Goal,' list at least one key piece of advice that will help you on your pursuit of achieving your goals.

Write the page number this advice is found so that you can reference back when achieving future goals.

Plan Accordingly

_____

_____

Remove Distractions

_____

_____

Remove Idols

_____

_____

Set Professional and Personal Boundaries

_____

_____

_____

_____

Use Discretion

_____

_____

Seek Wise Counsel

_____

_____

Prayer

Father, thank You for sending Your Son Jesus to be an example for me as I pursue to do Your will in my life. I thank You that Your Son bore my sins on the cross and as a result You view me as pure and righteous. Help me to be a good steward of my goals during the planning and researching phase. Help me to realize all areas of improvement so that I can come to You with an open heart asking for Your strength and guidance. Help me to plan accordingly in preparation of pursuing my goal. Help me to remove distractions and idols that may have taken Your place. Forgive me God for ever putting something or someone ahead of You. Help me to determine boundaries personally and professionally so that what You pour into me spiritually can be poured in its proper place. I pray for discernment so that I can know who to share my God-driven goals with and to also have wise counsel to share my ideas with. I thank You in advance for all of the work You have done and will continue to do in my life.

In Jesus' name I pray.
Amen.

Chapter 5:

THE PURSUIT OF ACHIEVING YOUR GOALS

"I press on toward the goal to win the prize for which God has called me heavenward in Christ Jesus."

Philippians 3:14
NIV

THE PURSUIT OF ACHIEVING YOUR GOALS

Finally, the conversation about achieving your goals! *Nowww we can do the real happy dance. *Queue the Shaq Shoulder Dance Gif**

After you have determined your goals and have been a good steward of those goals, it's time to implement a practical tool to achieve your goals. We are going to utilize the *'Submit, Rely, and Obey'* method. Unfortunately, this practical tool doesn't utilize a same letter acronym but *'best believe'* it'll be just as effective!

SUBMIT

> *"Trust in the LORD with all your heart*
> *and lean not on your own understanding;*
> *in all your ways submit to him,*
> *and he will make your paths straight."*

Proverbs 3:5-6 NIV

The first step in the pursuit of achieving your goals is to *Submit*. You will fully *submit* and surrender your plans to God through prayer. You're probably thinking, *"Meli I already prayed! I determined goals and prayed about it. I was a good steward and developed plans of action and prayed about it. And now you're telling me on the pursuit of achieving my goals I have to pray about it again?"* **Yep.**

One of the high school girls that I mentor in my church youth group, told me that a family member asked, *"Why is there a need for prayer?"* If we have faith to believe that God works all things out for our good (as stated in Romans 8:28) then *why pray*? I could just answer you with, *"Because God's word says so,"* but you might have some brat-like tendencies (*like I do*) and would appreciate a deeper and thought out answer on why we are called to pray. I want to provide you with a little explanation about what scripture says about prayer.

In one of my favorite verses, Philippians 4:6-7 NLT, it says, *"Don't worry about anything; instead, pray about everything. Tell God what you need, and thank him for all he has done. Then you will experience God's peace, which exceeds anything we can understand. His peace will guard your hearts and minds as you live in Christ Jesus."*

Prayer helps ease our worry and anxiety and also helps posture our hearts to be joyful for all that He has already done for us. We get to experience His peace that is only provided from the supernatural source of the Holy Spirit (which we will discuss more in depth in the next section).

In 1 Thessalonians 5:16-18 NLT it says, *"Always be joyful. Never stop praying. Be thankful in all circumstances, for this is God's will for you who belong to Christ Jesus."* As believers, we should *always* utilize prayer in every situation. It is our line of communication with God and we should always keep that line open and constant.

And lastly, *"And we are confident that he hears us whenever we ask for anything that pleases him. And since we know he hears us when we make our requests, we also know that he will give us what we ask for."* (1 John 5:14-15 NLT). Prayer time with God is more than just a time to request things from Him, yet there are several supporting scriptures that imply that we should be specific in our prayers and this is one of them. God desires to fulfill our requests that are in alignment with His will for us. But when we don't even know specifically what we want, how can we determine that He answered our prayer?

I remember I used to be extremely vague in my prayers and I would pray those *'cute'* prayers. *Y'all know what I'm talking about.*

Those short, simple, and sweet ones. *"Lord lead me on the path to success today. Amen."* It was almost like my husband's go-to prayer before our food, *"God is great. God is good. Lord thank you for our food. Amen."* I admit, sometimes, I'm okay with this because 'ya girl' can get 'hangry' at times.

But why would we want a basic, cute and vague prayer when it comes to pursuing a great purpose for the Kingdom of God? Prayer will remain essential in our walk with Christ and your submission of your goals to God is out of pure reverence and honor to His holiness. Here's an example of being specific in our goal-setting prayers:

"Lord, I planned and determined my goals but I fully and entirely submit them to you. I want your will to be done in my life. I want this goal to lead me closer to the specific calling you have predestined for me to walk in. Lord, reveal to me if this goal is not in your will as I put all of my trust in your decision. Please confirm with me through your Word, a Spirit led brother or sister in Christ, or through the Holy Spirit if I am to proceed with this goal. In Jesus' Name, I pray. Amen."

Allow this moment of prayer, or series of prayers (it may take time before God answers) to be a deciding factor of whether or not you will fully pursue your goal by listening for God's instruction. Commit to discerning His voice, to listen for his *'Yes' or 'No'*. Look for His answer in confirmation through others in the faith. God may answer you in a gentle, quiet voice or He may use the body of Christ to speak to you. So pay attention!

If you see a 'sign' that you *feel* is God providing a 'Yes' to proceed with your desired goal, I still encourage you to take this before God in prayer. The enemy is known to sometimes send 'counterfeit' things in our lives so assure it truly is God.

"But I am not surprised! Even Satan disguises himself as an angel of light." (2 Corinthians 11:14 NLT).

To further explain, I want to bring up another great sermon from Pastor Michael Todd from his 'Crazy Faith' series which was on the topic of "Hasty Faith." The term *'hasty faith,'* which defined from his sermon, is faith in action but moving too quickly and before God's timing. He explained about Saul's 'hasty faith' found in 1 Samuel 13: 5-13. During this time, Saul was Israel's King and was anointed by a prophet named Samuel. Saul's army was preparing for battle against the Philistines and was instructed by the Lord to wait for Samuel to arrive where they were. Samuel would then sacrifice an offering to the Lord so that they would obtain favor and victory against the enemy. Once Saul was under pressure from his army, he did not heed the instruction and acted in fear and anxiety by offering the sacrifice himself. Samuel arrived shortly after Saul's 'hasty' decision and rebuked him for his disobedience.

What I'd like to instill as encouraging advice for you Goal-Getters is to not pursue your goals out of pressure, fear, and/or anxiety. If God is telling you to wait before pursuing, then yield to His instruction. This stage will require discerning of His voice and trusting in His timing. Once you have received God's 'Yes' then you will utilize the proceeding tools in correlation with pursuit. We truly are balancing our ambition and submission, by utilizing practical work and effort along with submission through prayer. We want to assure heeding His voice prior to moving forward so we can be in willful obedience to the Father.

SUBMIT YOUR DAILY LIFE TO HIM

*"If you cling to your life, you will lose it;
but if you give up your life for me, you will find it."*

Matthew 10:39 NLT

There could be a potential of getting caught up in the pursuit of our goals that we could fail to *remain submitted* to Christ. We could choose to keep our plans in life without *any* submission to Him, but if we did, we would end back in selfish striving and not truly being fulfilled or satisfied in our life. *"For the world offers only a craving for physical pleasure, a craving for everything we see, and pride in our achievements and possessions. These are not from the Father but are from this world. And this world is fading away, along with everything that people crave. But anyone who does what pleases God will live forever."* (1 John 2:16-17 NLT).

I love that Jesus says that when we are willing to *give up our life for Him*, we will find 'it.' As backwards as it sounds, our willingness to loosen our grip on earthly rewards (power, popularity, material possessions, etc.) frees us up to submit and follow Christ. Through that submission, it will cause us to *find* our life and essentially find the purpose that many are desperately searching for.

I encourage you to seek God daily and ask if there is an opportunity for you to be used for His glory. These small 'tasks' could very well be character building blocks to grow you, change you, and fulfill the purpose we have as believers through loving others with faith in action.

Submit your goals to the Lord, remain submitted to Him daily, and rest assured that He will direct you if you need to adjust your goals to better fit the calling that He has on your life.

REFLECTION

- Did you receive any additional insight on why we, as believers, are called to pray? If so, what did you learn?

- After you submitted your goal to the Lord in prayer, what response did God provide? Did you receive confirmation to proceed with His 'Yes' or did you feel Him direct you to **not** pursue your desired goal? How did God confirm proceeding (through His Word, Spirit led brothers and sisters in Christ or Holy Spirit's soft, still voice)?

    I encourage you to ask for clarity and clear direction if God called you to **not** pursue your desired goal. His 'No' could mean, 'not now'. You might revisit Chapter 3 to utilize the Three C's to Determining Your Goal.

- How are you submitting to Christ daily? How will you release control over earthly rewards and allow God to direct you?

- When was the last time God provided an assignment for you to fulfill? Looking back, what were some take-a-ways? How did it help build your character and your faith?

Rely

"That's why I work and struggle so hard, depending on Christ's mighty power that works within me."

Colossians 1:29 NLT

The second step in the pursuit of achieving our goals is to **Rely**. Relying (or dependency) upon the Lord will always be a constant reoccurrence in our life. The definition of rely is, *"to depend on with **full trust or confidence**."*[1]

Yikes. If I'm being honest, I can't really say I have **full** trust or confidence all of the time. There are times when my faith gets shaken, things don't go as planned, and doubt comes creeping in. And sometimes it becomes settled for a lot longer than I'd like to admit. But regardless of my emotions and feelings, that does not change the character of God and the promises that He gave to us. I have to lean on the truth of *who* God is, not how I *feel* God is due to my circumstances.

One of my favorite characteristics of God is His faithfulness. 2 Timothy 2:13 NIV says, *"If we are faithless, He remains faithful, for He cannot deny Himself."* Regardless of whether my faith waivers, I grow distant, or just become *'straight up'* disobedient- nothing changes who God is. I have to rest on who He is and rely on Him, not only for the pursuit of achieving my goals, but for all areas of my life.

Aside from our effort to fully rely on God, we should be encouraged that we also have God's Spirit, the Holy Spirit, Who we can rely on.

Rely on the Holy Spirit

"Nevertheless I tell you the truth. It is to your advantage that I go away; for if I do not go away, the Helper will not come to you; but if I depart, I will send Him to you."

John 16:7 NKJV

It's important to recognize that the Holy Spirit is the Spirit of God dwelling in us to help us, guide us, and direct us. It's a gift from God when we put our faith and hope in Jesus Christ (see Ephesians 1:13-14). As Christians, we believe in the Holy Trinity: God the Father, the creator of the universe and all things; God the Son, Jesus Christ who was God in human form who sacrificed His life for all of humanity's sins; and God the Holy Spirit provided to all believers who acknowledge that Jesus Christ is Lord.

The Holy Spirit has various nicknames in different versions of scripture. In the New King James Version, the Holy Spirit is referred to as *"The Helper."* In other translations, the Holy Spirit is described as *"The Advocate"* and *"The Comforter."* However, the original Greek word is the same, *paraklētos*, which is defined as, *"an intercessor, and in the widest sense a helper, succorer, or assistant."*[2] Although there are various synonyms for the word "Holy Spirit," it doesn't change Who the Holy Spirit is or His purpose.

The Holy Spirit will help connect things on a deeper level to our mind, heart, and spirit. Have you ever had a time where you were prompted to do something or led to something for 'some reason'? Well, often times that reason is the work and empowering of the Holy Spirit. *"No one can know a person's thoughts except that person's own spirit, and no one can know God's thoughts except God's own Spirit. And we have received God's Spirit (not the world's spirit), so we can know the wonderful things God has freely given us."* (1 Corinthians 2:11-12 NLT).

So how are we going to *Rely* on the Holy Spirit for our God-given goals? We will do this in two ways: relying upon His *wisdom and strength*.

THE HOLY SPIRIT'S WISDOM

After we have submitted our plans to the Lord, we will utilize wisdom from the Holy Spirit to reshape and perfect our determined goal. Because we have gone through the process of acknowledging that our goal is God-driven, assured it lines up with the Word of God, and have committed to being a good steward of the planning process, now we will allow the knowledge of God to perfect and refine the goal as needed.

After launching my monthly fasting meeting, the Holy Spirit began to reveal how to reshape the structure of the meeting. I originally planned for my meeting to be focused heavily on denying the flesh and declaring God's word over our fasting purpose. But it was through the impartation of the Holy Spirit's wisdom, that provided me with deeper insight on how to better educate on fasting.

The Holy Spirit led me to different scriptures confirming how fasting is a form of humbling oneself before God. At my meetings, I educate how fasting can posture our heart to *receive* the promises of God rather than believing that the act of fasting itself would *cause* God to fulfill those promises.

Each month as I prepare for my meeting, I rely upon the Holy Spirit as I study, ponder, and pray over which scripture to discuss. Out of a selection of two or three scriptures, the Holy Spirit provides a sense of direction or the 'instinctive' choice by being more drawn to one over another.

During the pursuit of your goal, allow the Holy Spirit to guide you, direct you and provide you with wisdom on how to reshape your original structure. Trust that the Holy Spirit will provide the wisdom of God and will make pursuing your goal that much more efficient.

STRENGTH FROM THE HOLY SPIRIT

The second way to *Rely* on the Holy Spirit is to rely on His supernatural power and strength. Many of us have heard the scripture that says, *"I can do all things, through Christ who strengthens me."* (Philippians 4:13 NKJV). Unfortunately, this is another scripture that gets misinterpreted. These words from Paul were written as encouragement to the church of Philippi, specifically talking about finding contentment in life. Whether or not Paul had plenty or was in need, he knew that he could truly overcome each situation with the power of God.

Now the Lord won't give you supernatural strength to *'all of a sudden'* be a national award-winning athlete (*imagine how many Kingdom builders would be top draft picks!*) but it should encourage you that the Holy Spirit can provide you with a supernatural strength to *persevere*.

Persevering means to 'stay the course' and *remain steadfast in the face of difficulty*. Perseverance is essential for successful living. It allows us to consistently pursue a goal or unwaveringly live out our beliefs, regardless of obstacles or difficulties.[3]

"Not only so, but we also glory in our sufferings, because we know that suffering produces perseverance; perseverance, character; and character, hope. And hope does not put us to shame, because God's love has been poured out into our hearts through the Holy Spirit, who has been given to us."

Romans 5:3-5 NIV

The goal you may have determined could very well be something that you need to invite the Holy Spirit to empower you. You might hit obstacles, roadblocks, disappointments, or stretch yourself to something you hadn't committed to pursuing before, but the Holy Spirit's strength and power will help you persevere yielding greater character and hope.

DO NOT GRIEVE THE HOLY SPIRIT

"And do not grieve the Holy Spirit of God, with whom you were sealed for the day of redemption."

Ephesians 4:30 NIV

I want to leave you with final words of advice in the *Rely* section on how to truly receive the best insight from the Holy Spirit. Do not grieve the Holy Spirit. You might be asking, *"Meli what does that mean?"* Don't tolerate sin in your life and be sure to release harsh feelings (such as anger, bitterness, unforgiveness, or even pride) from your heart.

My favorite author, Stormie Omartian, wrote in *"Lead Me Holy Spirit"*:

"We grieve the Holy Spirit when we think, say, or do things that are not holy the way He is holy. When we commit sin in our actions, words, or thoughts—such as when we are unforgiving toward another—the Holy Spirit is grieved, just as you would be grieved if one of your children refused to forgive another of your children. You would have grief over that until it was made right. However, if we are led by the Spirit in all things, we will never grieve Him." [4]

I felt challenged when I read her book because it made me reflect on my actions and motives. I desire to fully and entirely allow the Holy Spirit to work through me and reading the words written by Omartian were the convictions I needed even in the *'not so digestible'* truths.

I want you to understand that we won't be perfect and we won't necessarily be in a place where we may *never* grieve the Holy Spirit, but I want you to continue to allow the Holy Spirit to prompt you and convict you of areas to be attentive to. Search the depths of your heart to see whether there is a need to release some harbored negative emotions or attitudes. Ask God for forgiveness so that you can receive restoration and healing. If you are entangled in sin, confess your sin and truly repent, which simply means to turn 180 degrees and walk in the opposition direction. *"If we confess our sins, he is faithful and just and will forgive us our sins and purify us from all unrighteousness."* (1 John 1:9 NIV).

We want to invite God to reveal *anything* that could hinder The Holy Spirit's full manifestation in our life. The Holy Spirit truly is our Advocate, our Helper, and our Comforter. In order to fully *Rely* on the Holy Spirit's wisdom and strength we cannot block His fullness by grieving Him.

REFLECTION

- What level of trust do you have with God? How do you feel you can grow to develop your level of trust to **fully trust with confidence**?

- List at least three characteristics of God. What do those characteristics personally mean to you? Search scripture specific to each attribute to confirm the truth about His character.

- How do you think wisdom and strength from the Holy Spirit might help refine your goal? Make note each time you feel a prompting to reshape your goal and pray how it may be the Holy Spirit's leading rather than your own decision.

- Evaluate if you currently grieve the Holy Spirit. Are there areas of your life that you may need to confess - sinful habits and/or harbored emotions/attitudes?

OBEY

> *"Never let yourself think that you are wiser than you are;
> simply obey the LORD and refuse to do wrong."*
>
> Proverbs 3:7 GNB

The last step in the pursuit of achieving our goals is **Obey.** I first want to discuss the importance of our obedience to The Lord. *I don't know if you're like me* but when I hear the word 'obey', I feel a rebellious spirit rising up in me that wants to resist the feeling of having *zero control*. If you feel the same way, I want to provide some encouragement about obeying God.

When you obey God, you actually have *full* control in the decision you are making. You are intentionally *choosing* to be obedient to Him. Truthfully, obedience has been something taught and encouraged since our adolescent years.

Being resistant against authority begins at a very young age especially those *'terrible twos' (y'all remember...pray for us!).* Most of the time, this phase goes away around Pre-K or Kindergarten. Children begin to understand and obey the authority and direction of their teachers, yet the teenage years hit and there may be resistance against authority once again.

Some of us have grown into adulthood with a great deal of respect for authority, maybe even working in a position that would call us to lead or mentor others. However, there are others who have struggled with following the rules and commands of an authoritative figure with an adopted *"They-don't-know-what's-best-for-me, 'Imma'-do-what-I-wanna-do. 'Periodt'!"* attitude. *Queue sassy hand waves and motions*

Because of our human nature and earthly experiences, we can view obedience through some pretty *perverted* lenses. We could potentially view God as a drill sergeant barking orders and we are expected to say, *"Sir Yes Sir!"* We could feel obligated to obey without forming a loving and intimate relationship with our Father. This is often what *religion* or *legalism* might teach people rather than adjoining obedience and a loving relationship in one.

We could even think obeying God would lead to a boring miserable life. Thinking we will miss out on *'livin' our best lives'* could lead us to do whatever we *feel like* doing without any regard to God's desire, predestined calling, or penalty for sin.

Jesus said, *"If you love me, obey my commandments."* (John 14:15 NLT). In our walk of faith, we shouldn't choose to obey God out of fear or obligation from a religious requirement. Instead, it should be out of pure love for Him; desiring to make our Savior happy because He has done so much for us. So it's not that you have *zero* control of your life, you actually have *full* control by *choosing* to obey Him.

Now, how does a Goal-Getter utilize **'Obey'** in the pursuit of achieving their goals? Waiting for God. When God tells us it is time to step out, fulfill, and/or finalize our goals—we move.

During the *Submit* section: we submitted our goals to the Lord allowing Him to confirm proceeding with our selected goals. During the *Rely* section: we allowed the Holy Spirit's wisdom to alter, adjust, and refine our goals and invite the Holy Spirit's strength to help us persevere through the pursuit of our goals. And in this section of *Obey*, we wait for God's final instruction of when to *'Go.'*

Throughout this book, I used the example of my fasting meeting. I utilized the 'Three C's to Determining Your Goal' and the *Submit, Rely, and Obey* method during the pursuit of that goal. I *submitted* my goal entirely to the Lord receiving His 'Yes' to proceed, I *relied* upon the Holy Spirit to refine the vision and invited the Holy Spirit's strength to help me persevere during the months I've committed to my goal, and during the *obey* section, I waited until the Holy Spirit prompted me to '*Go.*'

I remember the moment when I felt the nudge and confirmation to '*Go.*' It was January of the new year, specifically the first Sunday, January 6th. Our pastor preached a sermon about making commitments to develop a closer and deeper relationship with God. At the end of the sermon, he asked us to do an activity. We were to write on a piece of paper: "What are we going to do? When are we going to do it? And Where?"

Immediately I felt the Holy Spirit speak to me, *"It's time to launch your fasting meeting."* Immediately, I wrote down all of the information on that piece of paper: *What are you going to do?* Host my monthly women's fasting meeting. *When?* The last Saturday of the month. *Where?* At my house.

The vision and goal were already developed, so when God told me to '*Go,*' all I needed to do was *obey*.

NOAH'S OBEDIENCE

I want to discuss a biblical character and his amazing obedience to God. Noah was a righteous man, blameless among people when sin was running rampant during that time, and walked faithfully with God no matter what. Because of the violence, chaos, and sin in the world God had a plan to flood the Earth, wipe out everyone, and essentially start over. Because of God's mercy, He chose to spare Noah and his family's lives and provided him clear and specific instructions on building an ark. *I mean seriously,* God was *extremely* detailed. He told him how large the ark should be, what material to use, where to put the door, etc. So, how did Noah respond to those specific instructions? *"So Noah did everything exactly as God had commanded him."* (Genesis 6:22 NLT).

Wow. Noah's act of obedience is beyond encouraging and inspiring. He didn't question or second guess God, but He simply *did everything **exactly** as God had commanded*. Now, there was a reward for Noah's obedience. His family would be safe from God's wrath and would receive the covenant promise that God would never flood the Earth again.

I want us to be encouraged that if we *obey* God and His commands that He will be faithful in providing for us. Now specifically *what* God will provide will be in question. It will be different for every one of us because we walk in different paths and are in different places in life. But one thing that remains constant is the pleasure God receives from our obedience.

A childhood friend of mine, Cierra Love Holt wrote *"ReRouting: Your GPS Never Fails."* She discussed her personal journey on how God rerouted her back on the path that would fulfill His will for her life. She heeded some advice saying, *"This journey takes time, patience, and obedience. You will be glad to know that you already have the map laid out in front of you. Now it is time to choose who is calling out the directions, you or God."* [1]

God is omniscient (*add that your vocabulary of the day*) which means 'all knowing.' Because we simply *aren't* God, we won't always comprehend why God calls us to do certain things at certain times. But we have to be willing to trust that He knows what's best for us and He simply desires our obedience.

Obey will be a key factor in achieving our goals. Constant obedience should be viewed as an act of worship, reverence, and love for Him. It's not an obligation or a manipulative way to receive what we want but a way to be fulfilled because we are doing the will He has for our lives.

REFLECTION

- How do you respond to obedience? Have you thought similar things like I have when it comes to the word 'obey'? Why or why not?

- How does the story of Noah and his obedience to God inspire you?

- When God tells you to '*Go,*' how do you think you will respond? Do you think fleshly emotions (such as fear, worry, anxiety, doubt) will rise up? Write down scriptures to reflect and meditate on to combat any fleshly emotions.

Prayer

Heavenly Father, I thank You for being my fuel and motivation to pursue my goals for the glory of Your Kingdom. I pray that You can help me to remain fully and entirely submitted to You. Help me to realize that by making the choice to lose my life that I truly find it by choosing to follow You and not the world and its rewards. Lord, I choose to submit my plans to You in reverence of who You are. Should You not want me to pursue this goal, just say the word. I only want the goals I wish to pursue to be fully blessed by You. Lord, reveal to me any areas that I may grieve the Holy Spirit so that I can name my sin(s) to You and receive forgiveness and restoration. I thank You Jesus that You paid the price for all of my sins, which allows me to be viewed Holy and Pure before our Father. I pray to be released from any bondage that might hinder the Spirit's full work to provide wisdom and strength along this journey. Help me to be fully obedient like Noah when you call me to 'Go.' I pray that I can set aside any hesitations or concerns and simply obey for Your Kingdom's purpose. Thank You, God, for the good fruit that will be developed after achieving my goals and the glory it will bring to Your Name. I pray that others will be blessed and led closer to You.

In Jesus' name I pray.
Amen.

Chapter 6:

Goal Building Blocks

"He cuts off every branch in me that bears no fruit, while every branch that does bear fruit he prunes so that it will be even more fruitful."

John 15:2
NIV

BECOMING MORE FRUITFUL

Being a Goal-Getter doesn't mean we determine one goal, achieve it, and then we are done. *Queue side head tilt* *You 'betta' quit playin'!* As we achieve our goals, they will become building blocks to even larger goals. Any successful entrepreneur first began with a vision and a goal, yet as they continued to achieve those goals they developed larger visions and larger goals. As mentioned before our intended purpose isn't to find success from a wordly perspective, but we should be encouraged that as we begin to achieve our God-driven goals they will develop into even larger goals laying out a more refined pathway for our calling.

Don't worry, you don't have to know your specific calling to set goals and achieve them through a Biblical perspective but it doesn't hurt to utilize practical tools and prayer to have a clear direction of how your God-given gifts and talents will be used for the Kingdom. (See page 160 for a self-evaluation exercise and guided prayer to help with determining your avenue/calling.)

As mentioned in Chapter 2, we are called to produce good fruit. When we achieve a goal, we may see the results and know that good fruit was produced, but it doesn't stop there. *"He cuts off every branch in me that bears no fruit, while every branch that does bear fruit he prunes so that it will be even more fruitful."* (John 15:2 NIV). Scripture says that he *prunes* the branch that **does** bear fruit for the purpose that it will be even *more* fruitful.

Pruning a tree is a 'real-life' thing and not just a metaphoric expression. I did some research on the act of pruning a tree because *'ya girl' is a city girl, remember?* A blog post *"What is Pruning?"* noted some key things about pruning that stuck out to me:

- "Sets the tree up with a good foundation for long-term health."

- "The goal is to remove unwanted branches, improve the tree's structure, and direct new, healthy growth."

- "When you remove old branches, you give trees the green light to put out healthy, new growth."

- "A proper prune is both an investment in the long-term health of your plants and in the overall look and safety of your property." [1]

Wow. We can definitely relate *the physical act* of pruning to our spiritual walk with the Lord:

- Jesus Christ is our firm foundation which causes us to have eternal benefits- while on this Earth and forever in eternity with Him and The Father (1 Corinthians 3:11).

- Our Father intentionally prunes us to improve our character and provide new and healthier perspectives to circumstances. Much like James 1:2-3 says that trials of many kinds produce perseverance. And through that we become mature and complete with developed character.

- After removing things from our character, we can begin to trust in our identity as being a new creation in Christ. The old is gone and the new is here (2 Corinthians 5:17).

- God is glorified when His children represent Him well. When we bear good fruit and when we become more like Christ during our time on this Earth (John 15:8).

When God prunes us, we are essentially being sanctified to be more like Christ. Sanctify simply means *"to be set apart and made holy."* Things are sanctified when they are used for the purpose God intends and lives according to God's design and purpose.[2] This process will naturally happen as we continue to grow in our faith and fulfill our purpose as believers. Pruning is going to be a continuous journey for us so that we can bear fruit in *all seasons.* I always think of the scripture in Psalm 1:1-3 NIV:

"Blessed is the one
who does not walk in step with the wicked
or stand in the way that sinners take
or sit in the company of mockers,
but whose delight is in the law of the LORD,
and who meditates on his law day and night.
That person is like a tree planted by streams of water,
which yields its fruit in season
and whose leaf does not wither—
whatever they do prospers."

"Whatever they do prospers." Talk about life goals. Well, there's no need to envy the person described in this scripture because we, as God's children, can obtain this.

This is why I remain encouraged by the words of Paul when he said, *"Not that I have already obtained all of this, or have already arrived at my goal..."* (Philippians 3:12), because as we abide in Jesus, the Vine, and acknowledge that God is our 'Gardener' pruning us, we can remain steadfast to see a continuous cycle of fruit bearing.

MORE RESPONSIBILITY

"The master was full of praise. 'Well done, my good and faithful servant. You have been faithful in handling this small amount, so now I will give you many more responsibilities. Let's celebrate together!'"

Matthew 25:21 NLT

We have to understand that with elevation comes more responsibilities. Before we are provided a *'level up,'* God has to know that we are good stewards with what we have *right now*. He wants to see how we utilized and cared for what He has already provided.

I remember my husband talking to me about an employee he manages. The employee that reports to him often complains of not receiving a promotion, yet they are unreliable. This person calls in often, shows up late, and when given a task to complete it is not done properly. Instead of receiving correction, they make excuses rather than learn from their past mistakes. Because they can't be trusted with their current roles in that position, they haven't received a promotion, which essentially would yield *more* responsibility. This scenario made me think about the story in the book of Matthew about the Parable of the Three Servants.

Jesus spoke often in parables which was simply stories to illustrate doctrine and lessons of spirituality. In this parable, a master was planning to travel and was trusting his three servants with his money while he was gone. He gave one servant five bags, another two bags, and the last one a single bag. The servants with five and two bags decided to 'put the money to work' and double what they originally were given. Yet the servant with only one bag hid the money in the ground.

A long time passed and the master came back and asked the servants what they did with his money. The servants with five and two bags earned double of what they were originally given. Yet the servant with only one bag said to the master, *"I knew you were a harsh man, harvesting crops you didn't plant and gathering crops you didn't cultivate. I was afraid I would lose your money, so I hid it in the earth. Look, here is your money back."* (Matthew 25:24-25 NLT).

First of all, if I was the master *(or boss in modern view of things)* and my employee told me I was harsh, telling me how easy I have things because I don't work as hard as the servants do and *then* listen to their excuses *(which is simply their projected insecurities)* on why they didn't do anything with the money I was trusting them with, *I would have been mad too.*

So what was the master's response? *To no surprise,* the master was upset, took the man's money and gave the one bag to the servant who had the *most* bags. *"To those who use well what they are given, even more will be given, and they will have an abundance. But from those who do nothing, even what little they have will be taken away."* (Matthew 25:29 NLT).

Much like my husband and his review of his employee, the fact that he can't trust them with the smaller responsibilities means he could not imagine promoting them and entrusting them with even greater responsibilities. That's how we should view God's approach to elevation. It's not that you need to 'hustle hard' and expect to receive a *'level up'* from God but you should be willing to utilize what you have and be willing to be a good steward of what you have been entrusted with already.

God will continue to provide more for us as our character is developed and we can prove handling the responsibility which we already have. I want to add, that each servant was given different amounts, *"according to their ability."* (Matthew 25:15 NLT). So, God already knows what would be too much for you to handle.

If he gives you a task and it feels difficult, understand this is a valuable test of your commitment and faithfulness. Don't expect elevation without an addition to responsibilities. When representing His Kingdom, He will always allow new heights of elevation to grow and develop *even higher heights* of our faith.

FAITH REQUIRED

> *"And it is impossible to please God without faith. Anyone who wants to come to him must believe that God exists and that he rewards those who sincerely seek him."*
>
> **Hebrews 11:6 NLT**

Faith is required as our visions, dreams, and goals grow and develop to higher levels. Scripture specifies, *"Faith shows the reality of what we hope for; it is evidence of things we cannot see."* (Hebrews 11:1 NLT) The level of our faith will determine the level of capacity that God can work in our lives.

Every part of our Christian lives will require faith. We are essentially saved *through faith* from the grace of God (see Ephesians

2:8). And as Hebrews 11:6 says, it requires faith to please Him. When we don't utilize faith, we are giving into fear and unbelief, which goes against the many promises of God.

It's amazing to reflect on the miracles that Jesus performed, and the common thread being linked to their faith. Jesus often said, *"Your faith has made you well"* (see Matthew 9:22 and Luke 17:19) or *"Because of your faith you have been healed"* (see Mark 5:34 and Luke 18:42).

Because of their faith in Jesus, the belief that He was *able to* heal and restore, was the connection piece of it 'actually happening.' Got Questions Ministries phrased this way, "The power of Christ was what affected the cure but His power was applied in connection with their faith."[1]

Now, there were still instances where Jesus healed people who may not have known Him such as the disabled man at the pool of Bethesda (see John 5:12-13) or the man born blind (see John 9:1-12) but those noted instances reflect the amazing character of God's grace. Jesus' healing of these men was not about their faith as much as it was about The Father's will being done.[1]

Hebrews Chapter 11 makes note of very prominent people in Biblical history because of their faith and obedience. Their faith fueled them to make decisions that appeared to be risky, foolish, and even against the standards of the world. Their faith fueled them to make decisions that appeared to be risky, foolish, and even against the standards of the world. But they simply trusted God and His instructions on what He was calling them to do. Their faith was why they kept their pursuit of *'pressing on.'* In fact, their faith was so strong that they were still obedient even when they didn't see their promises come to pass (since many of the promises would be revealed generations later).

Peggy Joyce Ruth wrote in her book ,*"Psalm 91"*: "Faith is not a tool to manipulate God into giving you something you want. Faith is simply the means by which we accept what God has already made available. Our goal needs to be the renewal of our minds to such an extent that we have more faith in God's Word than in what we perceive with our physical senses. God does not make promises that are out of our reach." [2]

Trust in God's word and His promises, the promises written for all believers as well as the ones He has given to you personally. Don't let past moments of your faith being shaken hold you back either. *"Forget what is behind and strain toward what is ahead..."* (Philippians 3:13). Let your faith be the connection piece to seeing God's work come to pass. Let's allow our dreams to grow beyond what we have already achieved.

REFLECTION

- How did the concept of pruning comparative to your spiritual walk provide deeper insight?

- How are you encouraged that the pruning process will help you yield more fruit?

- Are you ready for elevation even though it means more responsibility? How will you prepare for it?

- What promises from the Word of God are fueling your faith? Has God given you any specific promises? Make a list of those scriptures and promises below and refer to when you need a reminder along your journey.

Scriptures to Fuel My Faith

_____

_____

_____

Promises God Gave Me

_____

_____

_____

Scriptures to Fuel My Faith

_____

_____

Promises God Gave Me

_____

_____

Prayer

Lord, I am amazed at Your goodness and glory in my life. I thank You God for all you have done and will continue to do. I thank You that You desire for us to be fruitful in all seasons but that means that pruning will be something I must be prepared for. Help me to learn, grow, and develop during the stage of pruning and to be reminded that I am being sanctified to be more like your Son, Jesus. Thank You for not giving me more than I can handle, as You give according to my ability. Lord lead me to Your Word and promises that will fuel my faith so that I can see your miraculous work in my life.

In Jesus' name I pray.
Amen.

Chapter 7:

Watch God Work

"Then he said to them all: 'Whoever wants to be my disciple must deny themselves and take up their cross daily and follow me.'"

Luke 9:23
NIV

BE PREPARED TO GET UNCOMFORTABLE

The perspective from the world might set up a false concept that the pursuit of purpose will *only* be fulfilling and fun. Have you heard the saying, "Do what you love, and you'll never work another day in your life"? *Eh.* That *sounds good* but is that really true?

I think we have to set our expectations in the proper place. It may be true that you realize the work and labor is not going in vain and good fruit should be expected to follow but we can't neglect the fact that there will be work involved and it's not always going to be the *most comfortable.*

Jesus told His disciples, *"Whoever wants to be my disciple must deny themselves and take up their cross daily and follow me."* (Luke 9:23 NIV). Being a disciple of Christ means that we are going to have to crucify our flesh *daily.* Not just on Sundays after hearing an amazing church message that made you sob your eyes out because it felt like the message was directly speaking to you. (*Okay, maybe that's an example specifically about me. But let's just say, my false lashes have not been salvageable after some services!*) Although it's great to receive a deep message on Sunday, it's truly not sustainable if we aren't integrated with consistent, daily, sacrifice.

I love how John Piper describes what Jesus means in this passage *"Taking up our cross means Jesus has become more precious to us than approval, honor, comfort, and life."* Piper also says, *"You are a new self. Act like it. Deny the old, comfort-craving self and embrace the superior joy of knowing Jesus, no matter how high the cost on this earth."*[1]

Denying ourselves doesn't mean we *'straight up'* won't do anything that we think only benefits us like: shower, eat, brush our teeth *because Lord Jesus, please brush your teeth!*

But it means to be committed to Christ above all things despite our emotions or our feelings. Taking up our cross, means that we ought to deny anything that would draw us farther away from Jesus. We must remain steadfast in obeying His commands and imitating His life, so that we don't revert back to self-ambitious mindsets and the compromising of our goals based upon what's popular in the world. We must remain steadfast in obeying His commands and imitating His life, so that we don't revert back to self-ambitious mindsets and the compromising of our goals based upon what's popular in the world.

Goal-Getters, be prepared to get uncomfortable, but I promise, this journey will be well worth it.

CHARACTER IS DEVELOPED IN THE LONG ROUTE

As we have mentioned, there will be discomfort and stretching along this journey. You might desire to quickly achieve your smaller goals so that you can begin to develop your larger goals, but God might be calling you to determine, fulfill, and focus on those smaller goals first. It might appear to be a longer route, but we have to trust that He has our best interest at heart and trust that developed character will happen along the way. When I think about a slow journey and possibly even a longer route, I always think about the Israelites intentionally being taken through the wilderness on their route to the Promised Land.

"When Pharaoh finally let the people go, God did not lead them along the main road that runs through Philistine territory, even though that was the shortest route to the Promised Land. God said, 'If the people are faced with a battle, they might change their minds and return to Egypt.' So God led them in a roundabout way through the wilderness toward the Red Sea. Thus the Israelites left Egypt like an army ready for battle." (Exodus 13:17-18 NLT).

It was God's protection to take the Israelites the 'long route' to keep them from having to fight the Philistines. He knew that their mindset and perspective wouldn't be able to handle the battles ahead of them. His intention was to prepare them and develop their character.

The Lord did so much for them during their wilderness season. He guided them during the day by a pillar of cloud and by a pillar of fire at night, parted the Red Sea to rescue them from the Egyptians, made bitter water better for them to drink, rained food from the sky, provided water from a rock when they were thirsty, and the many victories against their enemies. *Wow, talk about God providing for them.* Unfortunately, despite the amazing provision from the Lord they still struggled and complained against God. *And let me tell you*, reading their story makes me think it was *like 'all day erryday'. I mean*, they always seemed to find the next 'thing' to complain about. They struggled so much so that majority of them ended up dying in the wilderness and never saw the land promised to them. It was, however, generations later that their offspring would inherit the land.

God revealed Himself time and time again to the Israelites. Everything He did was an opportunity to build their faith, but they kept looking at each circumstance, losing trust in God time and time again.

We always use the Israelites as an example of what *not* to do. I often hear people judging them and ridiculing how they could have so much lack of trust for God despite the amazing signs and wonders He did for them. But if we are honest, we too, can easily fall victim to the same pattern they did. If we don't allow our minds to be renewed and fix our eyes on Jesus instead of our circumstances, we can remain in a cycle of endless demanding of and complaining to God.

Don't make the same mistake the Israelites did by complaining and resisting. Don't remain stuck in old mindsets, patterns of disobedience, and in doubt of God and His amazing character. Follow God willingly on the long route to develop your character and be sure to ask God what it is He wants you to learn during this experience. Our Father wouldn't delay the fulfillment of our God-driven goals, that are in alignment with His will, *without* having a purpose in doing so.

Remember it was all for the Israelite's protection to be rerouted so I invite you to take this into your prayer time to ask what you can learn and develop in your character if you feel God is taking you the 'long route.'

GOD'S PROVISION IS A BLESSING NOT A REQUIREMENT

I have seen a meme shared and reposted multiple times that says, "He is not checking your bank account, He is checking your faith account." *I mean it sounds cute...* But how are you interpreting this? I think this interpretation can lead an aspiring entrepreneur to think that God will 'magically' drop $10,000 in their bank account as long as they have faith. I'm not saying God *can't*. Because, *Lord...if that's your will, I accept it, receive, and would be grateful!* But financial provision is a blessing, not something we should see as an expectation to do His will.

King Solomon was a very wise and rich king. He was the heir to throne from his father, King David. God appeared to Solomon one night and asked him what he wanted. He could ask for whatever and he would give it to him. Solomon said, *"Give me the wisdom and knowledge to lead them properly, for who could possibly govern this great people of yours?"* (2 Chronicles 1:10 NLT).

Now, Solomon had a great heart to only ask for wisdom and knowledge *because y'all...* I'm not saying I wouldn't have asked for something honorable. *I'm just sayin,'* I 'woulda' threw in there something extreme *(and probably unnecessary)* like *unlimited Starbucks or somethin', ya know?!*

Because of Solomon's honorable request, God was well pleased. He listed how Solomon could have asked for wealth, riches, fame, death of his enemies or a long life but instead he asked for wisdom and knowledge to better serve His people.

"I will certainly give you the wisdom and knowledge you requested. But I will also give you wealth, riches, and fame such as no other king has had before you or will ever have in the future!" (2 Chronicles 1:12 NLT).Not only did God provide what Solomon asked for, He gave him financial provision of wealth, riches, and fame!

The material things were not a higher priority for Solomon than wisdom. By gaining wisdom, he would be able to pursue a greater purpose and be in alignment with God's Will to serve others.

I feel confident that as you continue to walk in full submission to the Lord that the desires of your heart will naturally be shaped to become more pleasing to Him. As your desires are reshaped, the concept of financial provision will take a *'back seat'* to asking God for more wisdom, clarity, and direction. Of course, to create and innovate different products or services to serve others, there will be a need for provision. But we should be confident that we serve a God who provides and has access to *every* resource at His fingertips.

I like the phrase, "Where God guides, He provides" because that technically goes back to the Word of God in Isaiah 58:11 NLT: *"The L*ORD* will guide you continually, giving you water when you are dry and restoring your strength. You will be like a well-watered garden, like an ever-flowing spring."*

This is much like the often-quoted, Jeremiah 29:11 NIV scripture: *"For I know the plans I have for you,"* declares the L*ORD*, *"plans to prosper you and not to harm you, plans to give you hope* *and a future."* Although there is still specific context to whom this scripture was originally spoken to, these scriptures can still be applied to our walk with Christ today.

What we can gather from those scriptures is that our submission to Him and our willingness to follow His guidance, will provide us with a promise that He will provide all that we need. I encourage you to ask the Lord for wisdom and clarity rather than financial provision itself. When our heart is to serve God, if we ask for His wisdom and insight to serve His people, financial blessings could very well be something given after seeing the desire to do His will. Remember, it is God's blessing but not a requirement for you to step out in faith and pursue your God-driven goal. If God has guided you in the direction to pursue a specific goal that needs provision, then seek Him, ask for His Wisdom, and allow the desire for finances to take a *'back seat'* to doing the will of the Father.

Rest assured that He will provide you with more than you ask for if your heart is positioned in the proper place. I have experienced God's amazing miracle work of provision and I feel confident that you can too.

REFLECTION

- Can you think of how you *deny yourself, pick up your cross daily, and follow Jesus?* Write down specific things that you have denied yourself from in order to be fully committed to walking with Jesus.

- Can you sometimes relate to the Israelites by looking at your circumstances and complaining against God?

- Reflect on one positive thing that God has done for you. How can that circumstance fuel your faith to develop better character? Ask God what He wants you to learn and what area of your life needs focused growth during this season in your life.

- How do you think asking for wisdom like Solomon can be beneficial to pursuing your God-driven goals?

Prayer

God, I thank You for showing me the way to be your disciple. Thank You for providing us Your Word so that we may know how it is to love You and to love others around us. Help me to remain focused on denying the desires of my flesh, picking up my cross, and choosing to follow You. I willfully choose to follow You all the days of my life. Help me to remain steadfast along this journey and to always keep my eyes focused on Jesus. Help me when I go through trying seasons, that You may remind me that you are developing my character and changing my heart and mind. Help me to always have a heart of gratitude for all that you have done for me. Lord, I pray for more wisdom and clarity in my life. I pray that the provision needed to accomplish my goals are provided and that I remain unfocused on the receipt of riches or fame. Lord I pray that as You provide more wisdom and clarity, it leads me down the path that You desire for me. I feel confident that all that I ever need will be provided from You, Lord.

In Jesus' name I pray.
Amen.

Chapter 8:

WHAT IF GOALS DON'T GET ACHIEVED
(LIKE YOU EXPECTED)

> *Look here, you who say, "Today or tomorrow we are going to a certain town and will stay there a year. We will do business there and make a profit." How do you know what your life will be like tomorrow? Your life is like the morning fog—it's here a little while, then it's gone. What you ought to say is, "If the Lord wants us to, we will live and do this or that." Otherwise you are boasting about your own pretentious plans, and all such boasting is evil.*
>
> **James 4: 13-16**
> **NLT**

WHAT IF GOALS DON'T GET ACHIEVED (LIKE YOU EXPECTED)

Welp, unfortunately I have to create a chapter about the harsh reality that goals *might* not go as planned and may not get achieved the way we anticipate them to. James wrote some harsh, *yet wise,* advice to believers. In James chapter 4:13-16 he basically says that we should be cautious about having confidence in our own set of plans.

> *"Look here, you who say, 'Today or tomorrow we are going to a certain town and will stay there a year. We will do business there and make a profit.' How do you know what your life will be like tomorrow? Your life is like the morning fog—it's here a little while, then it's gone. What you ought to say is, 'If the Lord wants us to, we will live and do this or that.' Otherwise you are boasting about your own pretentious plans, and all such boasting is evil."*
>
> **James 4:13-16 NLT**

Ouch. He's right, though. The reality is that God is Sovereign, holding supreme authority over all things. There truly is no way to manipulate, over-rule, or sway things to go our way no matter what we try to do. We might *think* we have control over things in our life but essentially God Almighty holds the true power and ability above everything. I'm going to take a few sections to discuss reasons why some goals may not have gotten achieved, and also offer a perspective if you did not yield results the way you expected to.

Trust God's Timing

"The Lord is good to those who wait on Him, to the soul that Seeks Him."

Lamentations 3:25 NIV

The submit, rely, and obey method is intended to help facilitate alignment with God's will and reliance upon His timing. But what if we misinterpreted when God told us to *'Go'* or we grew impatient with the time lapsed that we felt we must have 'missed' the confirmation? S*urely if it's been a long time then we just need to act, right? (Full sarcasm intended here!)*

Our timing is not necessarily God's timing and we really need to be mindful *not* to step ahead of God. I want to discuss the story of Abram (also known as Abraham) found in Genesis chapters 15-17. If you aren't familiar with Abram's life, I'm going to summarize this long story and provide some *"Meli'ed up" version cliff-notes.*

God chose Abram to become the father of many nations. He left his hometown and during several years of travel there was some opposition and drama with his nephew, Lot. We won't go into details about the drama with Lot but if you want some dosage of some *reality TV drama in Old Testament form,* check out the book of Genesis. *It is full of it honey*!

Abram gained great wealth over the years but spoke to the Lord about his concern of not having a son to pass an inheritance to. But much like our amazing Lord, He already had a plan and a promise. He promised that he and his wife, Sarai would bear a child. But *y'all*, he and Sarai were well over the age of seventy-five! *I couldn't imagine being anybody's momma at that age. Shew!*

About ten years go by after God revealed His promise and they still hadn't had a son. So, Sarai becomes impatient (*I mean she is super old by this time*) and decided it was best for Abram to have a baby with their servant, Hagar. During that time in history, it was custom for female servants to bear children on behalf of a barren wife, so Abram goes forth with the plan. *Happy Wife, Happy Life, right? I beg to differ on this story.*

Here's the rundown. *Takes deep breath in* Abram sleeps with Hagar, she gets pregnant, Sarai becomes jealous and treats her so badly that Hagar runs away, an angel appears to Hagar and comforts her, she comes back, and they bear a son and named him Ishmael. *Breaths out* Wheww. *Didn't I tell you this was a reality show fix? This is more drama than any real housewives could ever offer you!*

Since Abram had a son, he thought he was in the will of God. *Wrong.* Another thirteen years go by and the Lord appears to Abram again and reminds him of the promises He had spoken before. God told Abram that he would be a father of many nations and would bear a son who would be fruitful and multiply the land. This time, the Lord changed his name to Abraham and his wife's name to Sarah to represent that the time has now come to receive the promise.

Although Abraham already had Ishmael, the Lord told him and Sarah that they would bear their own son and the fulfilled promise would be made through him. Even though Abraham and Sarah overstepped and tried to force God's promise on their own timing, God was merciful and still fulfilled the promise through Abraham's son, Isaac.

What I want you to gather from this story is that God may have confirmed that your goals are in alignment with His will but we have to realize the fulfillment of any promise from God will be on *his timing, not our own*. A lot of pain, drama, and even future discord could have been avoided in Abraham's family if he and Sarah did not try to step ahead of God. Their actions displayed a lack of trust in God's promises and are an example of the havoc that can occur when we try to take things into our 'own hands.'

I want to encourage you to not step out of God's timing even if it feels like it's taking a long time. Sometimes, we are called to simply wait. As I mentioned before, I have some determined goals fully written out and ready to implement but God never specially told me to *'Go'* just yet. I trust that He will utilize those goals in the perfect time and season of my life. There could still be character traits to be developed in me, so as of now, these goals are left pending until the day He calls me to move.

LET HIS GRACE BE ENOUGH

> *"But he said to me, 'My grace is sufficient for you,*
> *for my power is made perfect in weakness.'*
> *Therefore I will boast all the more gladly*
> *about my weaknesses,*
> *so that Christ's power may rest on me."*
>
> **2 Corinthians 12:9 NIV**

God's grace helped me *so much* while writing this book. I had a goal to fully write the rough draft by a specific time, yet month after month would go by, and it still wasn't completed. It wasn't that I wasn't putting forth effort and intention to fulfill the goal, but there were circumstances in life that would cause a disruption to completing my assigned task. Some were spiritual attacks and others were simply responsibility of maintaining proper order as a wife and mother. *I mean I couldn't just say,* "Sorry hubby *and baby, I can't cook or clean for the next month because I need to focus on my book!"* That goes back to our *Commitment* portion of determining our goals.

Be mindful of your current commitments and responsibilities and remain a good steward of those roles. Even though I knew I was trying my best, I would feel disappointed when I failed to fulfill my commitment made to God. But despite my shortfalls, God gave me grace *each and every single time.*

The series of thoughts always circulated my mind: *"Could I have done more?", "Should I have done this instead?", "Or maybe (that)?"*

But the Holy Spirit always comforted me saying: *"My grace is sufficient for you. My power is made perfect in your weakness. Let me, alone, be enough for you."*

You see, the Holy Spirit's comfort (along with His wisdom and strength as mentioned in our *Rely* section) will always point you back to the Word of God. The comforting words from the Holy Spirit led me to 2 Corinthians 12:9. *"But he said to me, 'My grace is sufficient for you, for my power is made perfect in weakness.' Therefore I will boast all the more gladly about my weaknesses, so that Christ's power may rest on me."*

This was an opportunity for me to boast about my weakness so that Christ's power could uplift me, motivate me, and continue to fuel me along. It allowed me to rely on God for my effectiveness rather than on my own knowledge, gifting, energy or effort.

How often do we put expectations on ourselves to perform *perfectly* without fault? It's a guarantee that we *will* fall short at times and failure *will* happen at one time or another. But that's because we are human- imperfect beings. But here's a source of encouragement for you: *God designed us that way.*

God created us to always have dependency upon Him not just for 'things' but through an intentionally developed intimate relationship with Him. You may not realize, by admitting your weakness, it deepens your worship because you are affirming God's strength! The greatest gift of grace is Jesus Christ's life sacrifice for all of us but God's grace doesn't stop there. He continues to provide us grace throughout our journey of life, especially the pursuit of our God-driven goals.

We can set our goals and intend to pursue them but it may not go as we had planned. But, I'm here to tell you, that it's okay. It's a reality that we have to accept. I knew in my heart that I was doing the best that I could by balancing everything I had on my plate and God surely gave me comfort by letting me know *'it was okay'*.

If you have fallen short, give it all to Him. Surrender your feelings of defeat and guilt at the foot of the cross. He wants to comfort you. To love you. And remind you that *He is enough*. Allow His grace to be enough for you. And allow that hope to fuel you to keep *'pressing on.'*

THE WORLD'S VIEW OF SUCCESS VS GOD'S

We may not achieve the results that we anticipate *especially* during the pursuit of God-driven goals. You see, God's view of success may not be comparative to The world's view of success.

Many social media influencers view their success on numbers: number of followers, likes, responses; but that's because the larger the numbers, the more likely they will get sponsored by various companies. Even though we may not be taking the route of becoming a social media influencer, we still tend to feel the most validation through the higher numbers on our social media accounts.

After I put my faith in Christ, I completely reshaped my social media for the impact and influence to spread the Gospel. A fiery passion was in my heart to spread the goodness of God. I grew so close to Him and saw so many things change in my family and I that I wanted others to experience what I had. I began posting scripture and memes that talked about God, yet I was still heavily driven by numbers and followers. I was used to receiving a minimum of 100 likes on one of my selfies with a follower count of over 2k followers. *Now, don't roll your eyes and laugh if you're one of those '10k follower people' reading my book. 100 was a lot for me!*

But once I would post about God, I'd be lucky to get 10 likes. I wrestled with emotions of validation through likes but kept posting and sharing stories about things placed on my heart during my study in the Word. Even though I lost some followers and my likes were minimal, I had quite a bit of people message me displaying their thankfulness to my posts. They shared their struggles during that season but yet my post provided them hope, encouragement, and most importantly encouraged them to put their faith back in God.

From the world view, it looks as if I no longer have success because of the decreased likes, but I know in God's eyes, that touching at least one person yields a great deal of success. I think about the parable where Jesus leaves the ninety-nine to find the one lost sheep. *"In the same way, there is more joy in heaven over one lost sinner who repents and returns to God than over ninety-nine others who are righteous and haven't strayed away!"* (Luke 15:7 NLT).

I have to remain committed to serving God despite what the world advocates and teaches. And I want you to remain committed as well. Don't let the temptation to find things culturally accepted or the 'quick' route to fame or numbers because that truly goes back to our intro chapter's discussion on pursuing God-driven goals rather than self-ambitious ones. The world will make you believe that it's all about you but we know that it's about God, serving His people, and bearing good fruit for His Kingdom, not our own.

"So let's not get tired of doing what is good. At just the right time we will reap a harvest of blessing if we don't give up." (Galatians 6:9 NLT). God will lift us up in honor in *due time* and others will see our success giving back glory to God in the end. For now, our role is to remain humble, remain committed to serving goals driven by Him and His word, and trust Him along the way.

BREAK FREE FROM COMPARISON

In our social media era today, it's hard not to compare. It's hard not to think that if someone else is yielding success in what *they* are pursuing for God that you will have the same results.

I remember seeing an amazing and talented lady who was pursuing the same type of pathway that I am led to, which is teaching about purpose and goal-setting. I would see posts from her events where she would have a room *full* of people. It would get me so excited that I couldn't wait until I would be able to share my posts and get everyone congratulating me. I wouldn't neglect giving glory back to God for my success. Well, let me share how my experience went with my monthly fasting meeting.

My first meeting for "Fasting with Purpose: A Women's Worship Experience" was held on the 4th Saturday of January, 2019. I decided to utilize Facebook and create a private event to invite people. For the very first meeting, I invited fifteen people. Five people marked 'Yes' and four marked 'Maybe'. I was hoping that two or three people would respond so to have nine people respond was *huge* to me! *Hey, bar was set low, okay?*

The morning of my meeting comes, and I made sure to wear my *"Woman of God"* shirt from God Is Dope Clothing Brand. *'Ya girl' was going to make sure she took candid shots to post for the 'gram'!* I was checking out the lighting and all of the logistics to where I would set my phone up so that I could get the *perfect picture.* I was even planning to add extra filters and maybe even an encouraging scripture and just be *'all the way extra'! Which if you know me, you wouldn't expect anything less.*

So the meeting begins at 10:00 am. Well, 10:00 am rolls by. No one's there yet. *That's okay.* I'm giving them a few more minutes just in case *they might be lost or something. Then it's* 10:15…10:30…and by 10:45, I knew no one was going to come. *Ouch. Talk about disappointment.*

I am typing this section at the end of July, which would make seven meetings held total. And to date, I have only had attendance at two of my meetings which only one person attended each one.

Even though I may not have an audience, and my track record has shown that it's a celebration to have at least *one* person attend, that hasn't stopped my commitment to this goal. Remember God's view of success may not always line up with the world's view of success. Also, the result of another person's goal may not always be the result that God intends for you to have.

Since God confirmed my fasting meeting through the practical methods discussed in this book, I am confident that I am pursuing this goal with a greater purpose. God's character remains the same regardless of my disappointment. He is All-Knowing, All-Powerful, and Faithful. My journey of being faithful to Him even when no one else is looking, has shaped my appreciation for pleasing God rather than receiving praise from people.

Regardless of whatever emotion you might feel during the journey of achieving your goals, I encourage you to bring it before the Lord and cast it upon Him. *"Cast your cares to Him, because He cares for you."* 1 Peter 5:7 NIV. The frustration, the confusion, the disappointment, the hurt – all of it. Just be honest. God is not surprised, I mean…He *is* God after all and knows everything we think and feel.

In order to truly fight our emotions, it takes surrender and resistance. Surrender (or cast) your emotions to Him and make the intentional choice to trust in God instead of your feelings. Remember in our *Know Your Identity* section (see page 20) to *take every thought captive and make it obedient to Christ* (2 Corinthians 10:5).

You can't compare someone else's results to what your results may be. In the end, comparison is a root of envy that will harbor in our hearts and will grieve the Holy Spirit. We want the full flow of the Holy Spirit in our life, so bring this immediately to the Lord, repent, and ask for a heart of gratitude and contentment regardless of your results. If God confirmed your goal, then the results are exactly how God intended it to be. So, *keep 'pressing on.'*

Reflection

- Are you willing to wait for God's timing, no matter how long it takes? How does the story of Abraham and Sarah remind you of the importance to yielding to God's timing?

- Do you remember a time when you fell short of an intended goal? How can God's grace *be sufficient* for you?

- How might your God-driven goals yield different results than something culturally popular?

- How can comparison harbor the root of envy in your heart? Anytime you notice you are comparing yourself to someone else's life, immediately repent, pray for blessings upon them, and ask God to provide you with a heart of contentment.

Prayer

Lord, forgive me for doubting You and allowing my faith to be shaken. I admit that I feel disappointed in the results that I have yielded but I thank you for Your comfort and Your Word that reminds me that it's okay. Help me God to trust Your timing, not my own. Help me to put my entire trust on when you tell me to move, and to not utilize human logic with my decisions. Father, I thank You for Your amazing gift of grace. Because of Your grace, I have salvation through Jesus Christ and Your grace will be sufficient during my weakest moments. Remind me, Lord, that "with man this impossible but with God all things are possible." I depend fully and entirely on You Lord. I pray that I can be broken free from the spirit of comparison and that I can fully trust that my results are exactly how You intended them to be. Remove the temptation for me to follow culturally accepted things and, should it come my way, help me to remain focused on staying true to pursuing the path You have ordained for me. I thank You, Lord, for Your patience and Your continuous grace.

In Jesus' name I pray.
Amen.

Outro:

Summary and Encouragement

"That is why we never give up. Though our bodies are dying, our spirits are being renewed every day. For our present troubles are small and won't last very long. Yet they produce for us a glory that vastly outweighs them and will last forever! So we don't look at the troubles we can see now; rather, we fix our gaze on things that cannot be seen. For the things we see now will soon be gone, but the things we cannot see will last forever."

2 Corinthians 4:16-18
NIV

Outro: Summary & Encouragement

So, here we are. At the end. I truly pray that the chapters in this book, the practical tools, and the Biblical stories discussed have provided great insight and direction to determining and achieving your God-driven goals. I'd like to recap the key points to serve as a quick reminder as you continue to utilize this book for the years to come.

How to be a Goal-Getter:

Chapter 1: Assure your goals are God-driven and not of selfish ambition. This can be determined by:

- Identifying if there is a 'root issue' driving your ambition.
- Knowing your identity in Christ and identifying as a Child of God above all things.
- Choosing to build God's Kingdom rather than trying to build your own.
- Demolishing mental strongholds by realizing the lies of the enemy and putting on the full armor of God.
- Studying God's Word to utilize interpretation and comprehension.
- Choosing to renew your mind by taking your thoughts captive, making it obedient to Christ, and meditating on God's Word.

Chapter 2: You are called to bear Good Fruit. In order to do so:

- Be honest and determine how good your soil is, which is the condition of your heart.
- Prepare your soil through: the Word, Worship, and Prayer.
- You can't bear good fruit without your connection to the vine, which is Jesus Christ. So abide in Him.

Chapter 3: Determine your goals through the three C's:

- *Commitment-* Take into consideration your season and roles to how committed you can be towards your goal. Think of this commitment not only to yourself but also to God.
- *Consistency-* What sort of consistent routine can you develop to fully commit to your goal? Remember to have consistent time with God as well.
- *Christ-* How does your goal line up with the Word and your intimate relationship with Him? Will this goal draw you closer or farther away from your personal relationship with Christ?

Chapter 4: Be a good steward of your goal by:

- Planning accordingly
- Removing distractions and idols
- Setting professional and personal boundaries
- Sharing your goals with discretion

- Seeking wise counsel

Chapter 5: Pursue achieving your goals through the method of:

- *Submit-* Submit your goal through prayer to allow God to confirm His 'Yes' on proceeding. Remain submitted to God daily by asking what He is calling you to do for the day.
- *Rely-* Rely on God with trust and confidence because of His character. Rely on the Holy Spirit's wisdom and strength and do your best not to grieve The Holy Spirit.
- *Obey-* Wait for God's command to 'Go' and remain obedient to His commands.

Chapter 6: As you achieve your goals, allow those goals to be building blocks to larger goals. Through that process you are:

- Called to be more fruitful, so expect pruning. The pruning stage will be uncomfortable but necessarily to yield fruit in 'all seasons' and to be sanctified to be more like Christ.
- If you anticipate elevation, expect more responsibility. After you have been a good steward of what you currently have, God can begin to trust you with more.
- It is impossible to please God without faith. So remain focused on growing your faith. The level of your faith will determine the capacity that God can provide larger visions and goals.

Chapter 7: Watch God work; but don't forget the following:

- Be prepared that *'denying ourselves, picking up our cross daily, and choosing to follow Him'* may be uncomfortable.

- God may intentionally guide us to determine and focus on smaller goals because He is taking us the 'long route.' If He is, He is doing that out of protection as He is developing our character and preparing us for future endeavors.

- His provision is a blessing but should not be viewed as an expectation to step out in faith. Focus less on the financial provision and more on gathering wisdom and clarity. As our heart becomes postured in the proper place, God will provide all that we need *and more*.

Chapter 8: And, in spite of all of the tools provided, the harsh reality is that there is a potential for goals to not be achieved as we anticipated. But be encouraged that:

- God is Sovereign. Nothing we do can *ever* manipulate a plan that He would not allow in our lives. We have to trust His timing and not our own. Also be reminded of the importance of not stepping *ahead* of God. A lot of pain, drama, and discord could happen if we do.

- Let God's grace be enough. He is and *always will be* enough for all situations in our lives. We most likely will fail and fall short of our intended goals, but God desires our dependency and His strength *will* be made perfect in our weakness.

- The view of success from the world may not be the view of success for God's Kingdom. Resist the temptation to turn to culturally accepted 'things' and remain committed to His pathway.

- Break free from comparison and release the envy from your heart. If God confirmed your goal, then your results will be exactly how He intends them to be. If you are disappointed, be honest with God, and keep *'pressing on.'*

A WORD OF ENCOURAGEMENT

Now that you are at the end of this book, I want to congratulate you on your hard work! No matter if you read this book entirely through before determining and achieving your goals, or you worked alongside this book, it still took commitment, consistently, and the fuel of Christ for you to complete this. *Tada!* You ended up achieving a goal that you may not have intentionally determined. *Look at you, bein' a Goal-Getter and stuff!*

I want to remind you from the introduction of this book about our foundational scripture in Philippians 3:12-14.

> *Not that I have already obtained all this,*
> *or have already arrived at my goal,*
> *but I press on to take hold of that*
> *for which Christ Jesus took hold of me.*
> *Brothers and sisters, I do not consider myself*
> *yet to have taken hold of it.*
> *But one thing I do: Forgetting what is behind*
> *and straining toward what is ahead,*
> *I press on toward the goal to win the prize*

for which God has called me heavenward in Christ Jesus.

Philippians 3:12-14 NIV

You *'pressed on.'* You realized there was more to obtain and you were fueled to pursue you God-driven goals. Allow those achieved goals to develop into even larger goals. You kept moving forward and didn't become stagnant. We don't celebrate old victories or get stuck in negative mindsets or patterns. We allow God to develop our character along this journey of being a Goal-Getter.
We will continue to press on to win the prize not for the glory and praise from the world but for the greater purpose of building for God's Kingdom.

I am so proud of you for being a Goal-Getter and wanting to pursue it through Biblical principles. I want to leave you with more encouraging words from scripture, a prayer from Paul to the Ephesians. This is a prayer that I have prayed over many people and I pray this over you as well. I hope you are encouraged, inspired, and that the discussions in this book fueled your faith to pursue God's Will for your life. Many blessings to you and to everyone you may share this book with.

Melissa M Simon

#MizzMeliInspires

"I pray that from his glorious, unlimited resources he will empower you with inner strength through his Spirit. Then Christ will make his home in your hearts as you trust in him. Your roots will grow down into God's love and keep you strong. And may you have the power to understand, as all God's people should, how wide, how long, how high, and how deep his love is.

May you experience the love of Christ, though it is too great to understand fully. Then you will be made complete with all the fullness of life and power that comes from God.

Now all glory to God, who is able, through his mighty power at work within us, to accomplish infinitely more than we might ask or think. Glory to him in the church and in Christ Jesus through all generations forever and ever!

Amen."

Ephesians 3:16-21 NLT

PRAYER TIME EXERCISE

Utilize the acronym of P.R.A.Y.

P-RAISE

Begin your prayer by praising God. Meditate on His attributes and His promises. Magnify His unchanging ways. Begin with adoration then go into thanksgiving of everything He has done for you.

Example: *"God You are Holy, You are righteous, and You are Sovereign. Lord, Your faithfulness is astonishing to me and I am forever thankful for Your unfailing love. Thank You, God, for sending Your Son Jesus to die on the cross for my sins. It is through His perfection that I am made pure. Thank You, God, for Your gift of salvation, as I could not have earned it, but it was something gifted to me because of Your Son's obedience. Thank You, God, for waking me up today and giving me the gift of life..."*

R-EPENT

1 John 1:8 NIV reminds us that we are all sinners. *"If we claim to be without sin, we deceive ourselves and the truth is not in us."* But be encouraged, verse 1:9 says, *"If we confess our sins, he is faithful and just and will forgive us our sins and purify us from all unrighteousness."*

We should search our hearts to reveal any sin that could potentially hinder the Holy Spirit's work. Then, confess our sins to God and allow Him to restore and heal those areas. This can be through unforgiveness, hurt, anger, sexual immorality, lying, etc. Repenting is not intended to condemn but instead to change (see Romans 8:1). Don't allow the enemy to deceive you with his lies and potentially build a mental stronghold. Instead, agree with God to refrain from committing a particular sin and you will see God's faithfulness to forgive and restore you.

A-SK

Here is your prayer time with God. *"Do not be anxious about anything, but in every situation, by prayer and petition, with thanksgiving, present your requests to God."* (Philippians 4:6 NIV).

This is where you can get alone and talk to God and ask Him for wisdom and clarity (i.e. about the particular season you are in to better understand the nature of the goals you are to set.)

"If any of you lacks wisdom, you should ask God, who gives generously to all without finding fault, and it will be given to you." (James 1:5 NIV).

Y-IELD

This is where you are to be still and listen. I encourage you to have a journal and make note of any thought, words, or images that come to your mind. If you are unfamiliar with recognizing God's voice, I encourage you to write down anything that comes to mind and ask the Holy Spirit to provide scripture for confirmation.

SELF-EVALUATION
FOR THE AVENUE/CALLING ON YOUR LIFE

*"Do not conform to the pattern of this world,
but be transformed by the renewing of your mind.
Then you will be able to test and approve what God's will is-
his good, pleasing and perfect will."*

Romans 12:2 NIV

SELF-EVALUATION QUESTIONS

- What are your interests, hobbies, and passions? Why?
- Do you enjoy these things due to an influence from the world (i.e. because it's popular, because it's what everyone else likes, because it's what your friends like, etc.)?
- As a believer, we all have specific spiritual gifts that have been imparted to us by the Holy Spirit to be used to build up the body of Christ. Have you discovered what yours are?
- Has your gifting been confirmed by other godly mentors, friends, pastors?
- How does your spiritual gifting line up with your interests, hobbies and passions?

Self-Evaluation Challenge

- Evaluate 'the root' reason of why you have a particular interest or hobby. If you truly don't know why then ask God to help reveal if this interest was given from Him or from influence from the world.

- Pray to God for guidance on discovering your spiritual gifts. Then seek wise counsel from godly men and women you know for help on determining your giftings. Be watchful and listen to how God will answer your prayer—personally or through others in the faith.

- Take a spiritual gifts survey to discover how God has personally gifted you. Pray over your results and share them with a leader at your church, small group, or with a godly mentor or friend. God *will* give you opportunities to use your gifting for His glory and the benefit of others in the Body of Christ. Just watch!

THREE KEY THINGS TO GROW IN KNOWLEDGE OF YOUR CALLING[1]

1. Be immersed in God's word. View your interests, hobbies, and passions through the lens of God.

2. Know what your gifts, talents, weaknesses, strengths are. Utilize the Body of Christ to what they see in you and also ask God to reveal how He sees you.

3. Evaluate what problem in the world you are drawn to. How can your gifts, talents, and abilities be utilized to solve this problem in a Godly manner?

GUIDED PRAYER TO PRAY FOR A REVEALED CALLING

Heavenly Father, I come before you, exalting who You are. Lord, thank You for sending Your Son Jesus Christ to die on the cross for my sins. I thank You God for your gift of grace and your faithful love to each and every single one of us. Lord, I come before you humble and with an open heart. I bring all of my sin, shame, unforgiveness, and bad attitudes and lay it at the foot of the cross. Your Word says that because of the blood shed on the cross that I am forgiven. I pray for Your forgiveness God and the will to remain committed to living a life pleasing to You. God, I ask that You reveal to me my calling and gifting. Help me to know my spiritual gifts, talents, and passions and how they will be utilized to service your Kingdom. I pray that You provide me with clear direction on how the goals I wish to pursue will be the avenue of my calling. I thank You God in advance for answering my prayers and I pray that You can lead me to scripture and godly people who will help me discover and understand my spiritual gifts. Help me to utilize the burden I see in the world and how You will allow me to service Your Kingdom through helping those people. Thank You, God, for choosing me. For loving me. And being so faithful to me that you gave up Your Son to die for me. I am forever grateful. In Jesus' name I pray. **Amen.**

EXERCISE

Keep a journal and write down scripture, words, or thoughts that come to your mind. Continue to pray this prayer and make note of what God reveals to you each time you pray and how it helps with understanding your calling.

Honorable Mentions

My Mom, Dad, Step-Mom, Father-in-Law, & Mother-in-Law: I am so grateful that God made you my parents. I thank you for all of your love & support.

My Brothers, Ryan, Cyrus, Ethan and Sister, Kimberly: I am blessed to have such wonderful siblings. No matter the distance, you all will forever be in my hearts and I pray nothing but God's best for your lives. Sissy loves you all so much.

Cristina Pack: You are the most generous and thoughtful person that I know. I am so blessed to call you my best friend. I thank you for loving me, caring for me, and supporting me in all of my endeavors. I have learned to love people through your selfless acts and I hope you always feel loved and appreciated by me and my family.

Jackie Cole: I am so amazed at God's faithfulness to send me a friend who serves as a mentor, an encourager, a prayer warrior, and someone just as *extra* as I am personality wise. You have poured so much into me and I am forever grateful.

Cierra Love Holt: Who knew that a middle school friendship would come back 'full circle' to serve a mighty purpose for the Kingdom of God? I am so grateful that we have had the means to keep in touch throughout the years. It is no coincidence that God brought you back into my life at the exact time He did. Because of your journey of faith, you have inspired me in my own walk. You also led me to an amazing mentor & prayerpist, Destiny Thomas. Through your growth and your obedience, I have learned so much from you. I am so grateful to have you back into my life as a friend and sister in Christ.

CHEYENNE HADDIX: I am so glad that God moved our hearts and helped us grow so that we can come back together and unify in friendship. You are such a dear friend of mine and I am so appreciative that we get to experience life together. You will forever be my 'gem' and I'm honored to have such a loving and caring friend like you.

VANNAH BRAMMELL: Who knew that our interaction at Grace Christian's New Year's Eve service would blossom into a friendship? Thank you for opening up your home and inviting me to your small group. Your heart is so pure and genuine. It is so nice to have met someone who loves Jesus and would also love me in such a pure way. I enjoy our conversations about life and faith and I am so grateful that we get to share life together going forward. I am so grateful to have met you.

I thank every single person that has come into my life and helped me to grow closer to Christ. There are many, many more people I could list here but space does not allow it. Even if our friendship was only for a season, I want you to know that you have had a great impact on my life, and I am so very thankful for each and every one of you.

Goal-Getter Certificate

*"Not that I have already obtained all this,
or have already arrived at my goal,
but I press on to take hold of that
for which Christ Jesus took hold of me.
Brothers and sisters, I do not consider myself
yet to have taken hold of it.
But one thing I do: Forgetting what is behind
and straining toward what is ahead,
I press on toward the goal to win the prize
for which God has called me heavenward in Christ Jesus."*

Philippians 3:12-14 NIV

How To Be A Goal Getter

For printable copy visit
www.SimonHousePublishing.com

Name _____

Date _____

About the Author

Melissa Simon is a wife, mother, and most importantly a daughter of the One True King. She and her family currently reside in Georgetown, KY where she serves as a high school group leader on her church's student ministry team. She is an author, speaker and has ten years of experience working in corporate banking. She is also the creator of her monthly hosted meeting, 'Fasting with Purpose: A Women's Worship Experience.'

She often goes by the nickname of "*Meli*" which utilizes her giftings to "*M*otivate *E*ncourage *L*ove and *I*nspire" people. Inspired by Matthew 5:16, she seeks to encourage people to let 'their light shine' by their good deeds so our Heavenly Father can be honored and glorified.

She is available for booking at: BookingMelissaSimon@gmail.com.

Visit SimonHousePublishing.com for announcements, purchases, and future book releases.

Author's Current Worship Playlist

Fun & Lively
- Tauren Wells- Miracle
- Tauren Wells ft Elevation Worship- Echo

Slow Surrender
- Elevation Worship- Here As in Heaven Acoustic
- Elevation Worship- Worthy

Gospel
- Todd Dulaney- Victory Belongs to Jesus
- Marvin Sapp- Best in Me

Author's Book Mentions

Joyce Meyer, *"Battlefield of the Mind"*

John Bevere, *"Killing Kryptonite: Destroy What Kills Your Strength"*

Jen Wilkin, *"Women Of The Word: How to Study the Bible with Both Our Hearts and Our Minds"*

Alli Worthington, *"Breaking Busy"*

Stormie Omartian, *"Lead me Holy Spirit"*

Peggy Joyce Ruth and Angelia Ruth Schum, *"Psalm 91"*

Cierra N Love Holt, *"ReRouting: Your GPS Never Fails"*

Footnotes

Intro: Pursuit of Purpose
[1] Pew Research Center. "Religious Composition of Younger Millennials." Accessed: 20, July, 2019, www.pewforum.org/religious-landscape-study/generational-cohort/younger-millennial/

Chapter 1: God-driven or Selfish Ambition
[1] Piper, John. "How Can I Soften My Own Heart." Desiring God. 9 September, 2016, www.desiringgod.org/interviews/how-can-i-soften-my-own-heart

Don't Waste Effort Building Your Own Kingdom
[1] "Heir", def. N. 1.1.Dictionary.com, LLC, 2019, www.dictionary.com/browse/heir?s=t
[2] "Heir/*klēronomos*, Strong's G2818" def. Blue Letter Bible, 2019, www.blueletterbible.org/lang/lexicon/lexicon.cfm?Strongs=G2818&t=NIV. Accessed 1, August, 2019.

Demolish Strongholds
[1] Meyer, Joyce. *Battlefield of the Mind.* (New York, Warner Faith, 2002). Pg. 16
[2] Bevere, John. *Killing Kryptonite: Destroy What Steals Your Strength.* (Colorado, Messenger International, Inc, 2017.) Pgs 2-3.

Study the Word
[1] Wilkin, Jen. *Women of the Word: How to Study the Bible with Both Our Hearts and Our Minds.* (Illinois, Crossway, 2014) Pg 36.

Choose to Renew Your Mind

[1] "Renew your mind/*anakainōsis,* Strongs G342" def. Blue Letter Bible, 2019, www.blueletterbible.org/lang/lexicon/lexicon.cfm?Strongs=G342&t=NIV. Accessed 10 September, 2019.

Chapter 2: Called to Bear Fruit

[1] "Fruit/karpos, Strongs 4151" def. Blue Letter Bible, 2019, www.blueletterbible.org/lang/lexicon/lexicon.cfm?Strongs=G2590&t=NIV. Accessed 10 September, 2019.

[2] McKay, Burns. "Flower Seeds that Sprout in One Week." Updated 15 December, 2018. https://homeguides.sfgate.com/flower-seeds-sprout-one-week-60864.html.

You Can't Bear Fruit without Jesus

[1] Piper, John. "What Does It Mean to 'Abide in Christ'?" Desiring God. 22, September, 2017. www.desiringgod.org/interviews/what-does-it-mean-to-abide-in-christ.

[2] Piper, John. "I Choose You to Bear Fruit." Desiring God. 12 October, 1981. www.desiringgod.org/messages/i-chose-you-to-bear-fruit.

Chapter 3: Determine Your Goal

[1] Worthington, Alli. *Breaking Busy.* (Michigan, Zondervan, 2015.)

Chapter 4: Be A Good Steward of Your Goal

[1] "Steward," def. N. 1.1. Merriam-Webster Incorporated Dictionary, 2019, www.merriam-webster.com/dictionary/steward. Accessed 15 August, 2019.

[2] "Stewardship,", def. N 1.2. Merriam-Webster Incorporated Dictionary, 2019, www.merriam-webster.com/dictionary/stewardship. Accessed 15 August, 2019.

Remove Distractions

[1] "Distraction," def. N. 1.1. Merriam-Webster Incorporated Dictionary, 2019, www.merriam-webster.com/dictionary/distractions. Accessed 18, August, 2019.

[2] "The sin/hamartia, Lexicon Strong's G266" def. Blue Letter Bible, 2019, www.blueletterbible.org/lang/lexicon/lexicon.cfm?Strongs=G266&t=NLT. Accessed 18, August, 2019.

Remove Idols

[1] "Idols/'eliyl, Strong's H457" def. Blue Letter Bible, 2019, www.blueletterbible.org/lang/lexicon/lexicon.cfm?Strongs=H457&t=NIV. Accessed 20, August, 2019.

Seek Wise Counsel

[1] "Counsel," def. N. 1.1. Dictionary.com,LLC, 2019, www.dictionary.com/browse/counsel.; "Counsel," synonym. Roget's 21st Century Thesaurus, Third Edition, Philip Lief Group, 2013, www.thesaurus.com/browse/counsel. Accessed 25, August, 2019.

Chapter 5: Pursuit of Achieving your Goal

Rely

[1] "Rely," def. V. 1.1. Lexico powered by Oxford, 2019, www.lexico.com/en/definition/rely. Accessed 25, August, 2019.

[2] "The Helper/*paraklētos*, Srong's G3875" def. Blue Letter Bible, 2019, www.blueletterbible.org/lang/lexicon/lexicon.cfm?Strongs=G3875&t=NIV. Accessed 25, August, 2019.

[3] Various Authors. "Running With Perseverance." Focus on The Family, 21 November, 2016, www.focusonthefamily.com/parenting/running-with-perseverance/.

[4] Omartian, Stormie. *Lead me Holy Spirit*. (Oregon, Harvest House Publishers, 2012) Pg. 94.

Obey

[1] Love Holt, Cierra N. *ReRouting: Your GPS Never Fails*. (USA, Cierra N Love Holt, 2019). Pg 31-32.

Chapter 6: Goal Building Blocks

Being More Fruitful

[1] "What is Pruning? The importance, benefits, and methods of pruning" Davey Proving Solutions for a Growing World, 12 September, 2018, blog.davey.com/2018/09/what-is-pruning-the-importance-benefits-and-methods-of-pruning/.

[2] Bible Study Tools, Baker's Evangelical Dictionary of Biblical Theology, Accessed: 21, August, 2019, www.biblestudytools.com/dictionary/sanctification/.

Faith Required

[1] Got Questions Ministry. "What did Jesus mean when He told people, "Your faith has made you well"?" Got Questions. Your Questions. Biblical Answers. 18, December, 2016, www.gotquestions.org/your-faith-has-made-you-well.html.

[2] Ruth, Peggy Joyce and Schum, Angelia Ruth. *Psalm 91*. (Florida, Charisma House, 2010) Pg. 52.

Chapter 7 - Watch God Work

Be Prepared to get Uncomfortable

[1] Piper, John. "Deny Yourself for More Delight." Desiring God, 30, May 2017, www.desiringgod.org/articles/deny-yourself-for-more-delight.

Three Key Things to Grow in Knowledge of Your Calling

[1] Piper, John. "How Can I Discern The Specific Calling of God on my life?" DesiringGod, 14 November, 2007, www.desiringgod.org/interviews/how-can-i-discern-the-specific-calling-of-god-on-my-life.

www.ingramcontent.com/pod-product-compliance
Lightning Source LLC
Chambersburg PA
CBHW051400290426
44108CB00015B/2101